Revised and Corrected

THE DRIVING FORCE

Memoirs of Wartime WAAF Drivers
1665 HCU and 81 OTU

THE DRIVING FORCE

Memoirs of Wartime WAAF Drivers
1665 HCU and 81 OTU

Peggy Drummond-Hay

Foreword by
Group Captain Mahaddie,
D.S.O., D.F.C., A.F.C. & Bar

The Book Guild Ltd.
Sussex, England

The Book Guild Ltd.
25 High Street,
Lewes, Sussex

First published 1994
© Peggy Drummond-Hay 1994
Set in Baskerville
Typesetting by Ashford Setting & Design Services
Ashford, Middlesex
Printed in Great Britain by
Hartnolls Ltd,
Bodmin, Cornwall.

A catalogue record for this book is available
from the British Library

ISBN 0 86332 8695

1665 HCU
Heavy Conversion Unit
Stirlings and Halifaxes

81 OTU
Operational Training Unit
Whitleys

High in the velvet mantle of the night,
Alone with just the moonlight on their
  wings,
The majestic of the vast universe
Made them feel the presence of the
  King of Kings.
The nights were long, as endless as the sky
Night after night their nerves were Tightly
  drawn
And quietly they prayed he'd guide their
  homeward flight
That they may live to see the beauty of
  the coming dawn.

By J.Davis

CONTENTS

LIST OF ILLUSTRATIONS

Centre section photographs:

Peggy Drummond-Hay on her first leave in 1943

Jack Heuff, a Canadian soldier stationed at Selsey
   Bill 1942-3

Mark III Stirling at Tilstock

Marjorie Cliff, Tilstock

Marjorie standing on one of the mobile flashing
  beacons, Tilstock

Dingle O'Neill

Frank O'Neill, who was a despatch rider at Tilstock

Tilstock: Nicky, Peggy, Beryl, Joan and Corporal Henry

At Tilstock: all that remains of the Motor Transport rest
  room in 1986

Vernon with his navigator by the tail of their Lancaster

Ron, who was in the Royal Australian Air Force, in 1943

Rosemary's husband Mac looking at his radio set in his Stirling

Tilstock: one of our first reunions in 1969

Peter was posted to an island in the Red Sea called Kamaran.

FOREWORD

by

Group Captain (Hamish) T.G. Mahaddie,

D.S.O., D.F.C., A.F.C. & Bar, Cz.Mc., C.Eng. FRAeS, RAF(Retd)

I have read and enjoyed Peggy Drummond-Hay's memoirs of her service as a WAAF during World War II. I am delighted to commend this to all who suffered wartime involvement in any of the services and endured the drama and the hardship of leaving home at an early age to experience such a strange environment with all the rigours and common dangers associated with the macho world of the RAF.

Perhaps I can offer a simple sketch of an incident to illustrate my point. In the very earliest days before the war started our WAAF arrived at RAF stations in their uniform — such as it was — a tatty old raincoat dyed in several shades of nearly black; a tammy with an airman's cap badge; the rest of their clobber was civilian.

The girls came from every walk of life; some from the manor born, Roedean, etc. But the vast majority came from the solid average working or middle classes . . . the very root and branch of our heritage.

One such lass was from a farm in the upper wolds of North Yorkshire and on her first day at RAF Driffield she was assigned

* Women's Auxiliary Air Force

11

to the officers' mess as a batwoman. Shaking with fear and highly nervous, her first duty the next morning, was to take a tray of tea into an officer's room (a major in the Royal Artillery), the flak liaison officer. She hesitated in the middle of the room when she saw this huge figure lying on top of the bed arrayed in silk pyjamas — in regimental colours, of course. (He had obviously been out of the room to post a letter or something.)

The terrified wee soul had never been in a man's bedroom before but obviously felt she should break the ice and the best she could think of was '. . . I have brought your tea, sir.' But having got that out she felt she should add '. . . would there by anything else, sir?'

Before answering the major thought for a moment and with his hands behind his head he stretched his limbs and said, 'Oh yes, give my Sam Brown a rub up.'

The tray of tea crashed to the floor and the WAAF disappeared. She was plotted racing through Scarborough, heading north, shouting 'Mum, Mum, M. . . u. . . m.'

In writing this foreword I would also like to pay tribute to my own WAAF and in particular, my M T* drivers at RAF Warboys, who carried out the most difficult driving assignments normally carried out by airmen much older than themselves. They were the first on the scene at any crash and had to witness the horrors of a frightful burn-up. They were out in all weathers in the full range of service transport from tiny fifteen hundredweight vans to great three tonners and enormous petrol bowsers. They had to endure the full range of blackout difficulties and normally they were on their own with no assistance from their male counterparts.

I doubt if any of you who have served in Bomber Command will ever know how your Commander in Chief fought tooth and nail for all ranks to receive a Campaign Medal, but was bitter that he failed because peacetime government of the day would not recognise the full value of Bomber Command and its part

---

* Military Transport

in the defeat of Nazi Germany.

Please, dear reader, accept this seemingly impossible incident of starting a Stirling engine with a 'looped rope'. The character who introduced this ploy to start an engine must have been an old sweat from the Messpot (Iraq) days and it was called the 'bag-and-rope' technique when our mechanics in 55 Squadron, Baghdad, started our Wapiti aircraft.

I was fascinated with the description of the girls and their early introduction to service procedure when at first they were sworn in, had medical tests and other indignities, and I am reminded of my own early days as a would-be apprentice at Halton. I recall milling about with several hundred other fifteen-year-olds in the station's sick quarters and being ordered by a corporal to have a pee in a bottle, and he indicated hundreds of HP sauce bottles stacked on a shelf high on the wall and some wag was heard to say 'What! From here?'

Despite my twelve years service man and boy, before the war started, I still recall the uneasy shock that lasted all my years when we heard that one of our WAAF was killed at Driffield by a bomb dropped by a He 111 during the war in 1939. From that moment the WAAF and the RAF were oppoes-in-arms.

I was always amazed doing my rounds at RAF Warboys and seeing my WAAF at their work places whether in the workshops or MT section, or in the equipment compound, handling difficult and sometimes dirty items for issue to the station, or indeed struggling with some return Group or Command. You were part of a vast team and however agitated and disarrayed you appeared at your work place you seemed to be transformed, like Cinderella, each time the camp hop came around. After the magic of a hair-do, a dab of powder and a lick of lipstick, you became attractive young women once more.

You and your kind, Peggy Drummond-Hays of the MT sections were everywhere in the WAAF, accepted the challenge of service with all the hardships associated with the war years. You set a high water mark of achievement which has been accepted and sustained by those who followed in the WRAF

13

as we know it today. You can take pride in the traditions forged in times of war that are now cast in the foundation of the Women's Royal Air Force.

A TRIBUTE BY THE 'WOP' WHO DID THE DRAWINGS

Much has been written, and rightly so, concerning the deeds and heroism of our aircrews during the 1939-45 war. We should not forget, however, that they were backed up by thousands of lads and lasses of the ground staff. Without them, the flying boys would never have got airborne or down to earth safely.

As far as I am aware, no literary bouquets have ever been presented to that happy breed of girls known as WAAF's DMT — I say 'girls' as most of them were little more than that, being in their late teens and early twenties from all walks of life. Yet they drove anything and everything on wheels at any time and anywhere, often under difficult and even dangerous conditions.

As a wireless operator during my RAF stint from 1942 to 1947, my active service in the UK after training and before being banished to airstrips in the Pacific islands and Burma, was at SHQ Signals Tilstock and its satellite, Sleap, from 1943 to early 1945.

During that time, the units in our care were 81 Operational Training Unit with their lumbering Whitleys and 1665 Heavy Conversion Unit with the massive Stirlings. Both types were eventually joined by gliders. We 'Wops' coined a phrase: 'Leave 'em alone and they'll come home dragging their Horsas behind them!'

In the course of my various duties, I often came into contact with WAAF drivers and invariably found them to be efficient, smart and cheerful with the added bonus of most of them being

15

pretty! Without their dedicated efforts to keep things moving, the RAF would have ground to a standstill.

They worked hard, laughed a lot and sadly they also died, as evidenced by the account of a tragic night to remember at Sleap in 1943.

John Martin

Kettering

ACKNOWLEDGEMENTS

Many thanks to the WAAF MT girls of 1665 HCU and 81 OTU who have added their memoirs and also to Frank, our dispatch rider, for his contribution. Also to our old MT Officer, Flt Lt Burne who was at Tilstock with us. Many thanks to John Martin who has been a great help with the writings, cartoons and drawings. Thanks to Tony who gave me the initial encouragement to write about WAAF MT drivers and also to my husband for his help and advice generally. Thanks to Jim Davis for allowing me to include his poem; also to Bob Tweddle, whose story I thought would interest many people who had not read or heard of his discovery. Thanks to Ray Glass for his amusing story of Woolfox Lodge and also to Jim Carey for his story about swinging the props. Last, but not least, many thanks to Group Captain Hamish Mahaddie for his foreword.

PREFACE

We ex-WAAF MT drivers from 1665 HCU and 81 OTU have held a yearly reunion at a Hotel in Whitchurch for over twenty years. This town is the nearest to RAF Tilstock in Shropshire where we were stationed during the war. So armed with some memories from these gatherings, I decided to try to put together something on paper which would be of some interest to ex-serving personnel.

Our reunions are most enjoyable and although most of us are about seventy years old, it is these times in the RAF that we remember most and we reminisce with lots of photos and old documents. We also spend time on the site where we were billeted amongst the remains of the old camp. One of our billets was near the old officers' mess which has been converted into a luxury bungalow where a family now live. They always make us very welcome and give us coffee each time we visit; they call us 'ghosts of the past'! When I said to the 'gals' as we call ourselves now, that I'd like to try to put a book together and I'd like a story from each of them of their memories, they all said they couldn't do it but, after some persuasion, I managed to get most of them to write something about their service life. My own effort is longer and I hope not too boring. Luckily my mother kept all the letters I wrote to her whilst I was in the WAAF and I kept a few diaries during that period, so the dates and facts are more or less authentic.

The 1665 HCU drivers only stayed at Tilstock for about a year and moved as a unit to three more stations before the HCU was disbanded but some of us had made good friends with the

81 OTU girls over the years and have kept in contact. When our families had grown up Marjorie and Betty started a reunion and held it every two years but as we are all getting older, we now have it yearly! We hope it will carry on for some time yet! The original gathering was for WAAF only but now we include husbands who married some of the WAAF drivers. Our old MT officer Flight Lieutenant Burne and his great friend, Jack Bramhall PFO (Physical Fitness Officer), have recently joined us and as they are both over eighty they say each year that it will be the last time for them, but they still keep coming! Frank O'Neill, married to Dingle, was our dispatch rider at Tilstock and has never missed a reunion. He always sits at the top of the table to keep an eye on us all!

We seem to get closer to each other as we get older and we treasure these friendships very much; we were thrown together because of the war and it takes war to find such comradeship, which is difficult to understand unless one has experienced the conditions we lived under.

1

PEGGY DRUMMOND-HAY

September 3 1939 — Selsey Bill, Sussex

I was fourteen years and four months old when war was declared. We were living at Selsey at that time as my mother had let our house in Cheltenham and I was going to a private school in Selsey. I can remember 3 September very clearly. We had gone round to a friend's house to listen to the announcement that Neville Chamberlain was making at 11 a.m. We gathered round the radio and listened to his grim words that we were at war with Germany: Peace had not come in our time after all, as we had hoped, and as had been his belief the year before.

I went out of the house and sat on the beach. It was a lovely sunny day with a very calm sea and blue sky. As I looked across the waters to the Isle of Wight I can remember thinking — I wonder where my future husband might be now if I should ever marry! Little did I know that he was on the Isle of Wight then with his family at their holiday home. Many years after we were married I asked him if he might have fancied me then and he said it was unlikely as he preferred blondes; I was a brunette! My thoughts were interrupted as the first air raid siren sent out its warning so I dashed back to the house; it was a false alarm but it made us aware that war had started.

As Selsey began to prepare for war, we started to fill sandbags and the young boys and girls who were old enough to join up

21

began to leave the village. The school holidays were at an end and my mother decided we should go back to Cheltenham. I was very sorry to leave Selsey. It was a lovely, quiet little seaside village with very nice houses, a few shops, a cinema, several riding stables and lovely sands with pools that made it fun for children to play in. The roads were unmade with large holes so that when it rained it made great fun to ride our bikes through with our legs held up high. The private school I went to was called Broombank and was run by two sisters called the Miss Morgans. They were in some dismay over the girls who were keen on horses. We used to cycle to school with head collars in our bicycle baskets so we could collect a pony each to ride after school. They belonged to an old lady called Miss Scrimgeor who ran a riding school with the help of many young girls like myself. She was an amazing old lady who used to ride side-saddle on a horse called Joey. Paddy Saunders was in charge of rides and so on and there was an old groom called Coe.

So I was sad at leaving all this. Cheltenham was a more restricted place to live in, but luckily I did have quite a lot of friends there, and had also been to a private school there. My father, who was on leave from India then, (I had been born there but returned to England in 1930 with my mother) had hoped that I would go to Cheltenham Ladies College and I had taken entrance exams previously and failed, and was supposed to try again after extra coaching. He was very disappointed that I did not want to go, so when we returned to Cheltenham, instead of returning to the private school I had a tutor called Mr Ross and used to go daily to his house which was opposite ours. He had been a master at Cheltenham Boys College and was very Scottish; he had two spaniels called Dot and Dash. He was mad on indoor plants, which he had all over the house, and he solemnly raised the Union Jack on his mast every day at dawn and lowered it at dusk! His pride and joy was his silver Riley Coupé in which he used to take me to Tewkesbury when he wanted to row his skiff on the river, and leave me to study on the bank. He had one other pupil, John Henderson, who was always gazing out of the window so as not to miss any aeroplanes flying overhead; I often wondered if John joined the RAF, but we lost touch.

22

I wanted to do something towards the war effort so I joined the local fire-warden service and used to go on watch with Colonel Gale who was in charge. One night there was a bad raid and Pilley bridge and a house at the end of our road was destroyed. Ironically, all the people in the house were killed, having just come down from London to escape the bombing!

I had quite a few friends in Cheltenham, having been to school there. We played tennis, as usual, in Montpelier Gardens, went to the cinema and had tea in the Cadena Cafe on the promenade. The family in the house next door had three sons and also had a friend who used to visit them; Tony was just sixteen and had a motorbike*. As we became friendly he asked me if I would like to go for a ride on his bike but I told him my mother would have a fit if I asked her, so he used to pick me up at the end of our road out of sight of the house.

Two spinsters lived in the house opposite. They had a nephew to stay when he was on leave, who turned out to be a sergeant air-gunner in the Canadian Air Force. So they invited me to have tea with them to cheer him up and we became good friends.

Then my mother agreed to buy me a horse from a riding school near the race course, which I had seen advertised in the local paper. When I saw the horse I fell in love with her at first sight and we bought her for the large sum of £12. I did not discover the reason for her cheapness until I found that she would suddenly decide to go backwards and would continue to do so until she thought she had better go forwards again!

I soon got used to her ways and became very fond of her. Luckily a friend of my mother's had a field nearby of about four acres (which is now a housing estate) where I was able to keep Nimble. Tony, my friend with the motorbike, also had a horse which he kept at a farm his father had on Cleeve Hill. They did not live there but had a farm manager to run the place. There were some lovely rides to be had over Cleeve Hill. So you can see that as we were under age to join up, we were having more or less a normal time.

---

* They were all at Cheltenham Boys' College.

We had civil servants to stay in the house, as my mother preferred them to evacuees, but when the cook and maid decided to join up my mother let our house for the duration and returned to Selsey. Incidentally, the person who rented the house, was the well known Alan Cobham who was doing work for the war effort and invented 'in-flight refuelling'. I think he used our house for his staff. Tony arranged for my horse to be looked after at the farm and I said goodbye to my Cheltenham friends.

It was 1941 and we returned to a very different Selsey. The cliffs had barbed wire and pill boxes with large concrete blocks and land mines dotted about all over the beach. The village was full of the Canadian Army and a lot of the local boys and girls had joined up. Everyone was doing something towards the war effort, even if it was only growing vegetables in their gardens and waste ground. We had some Canadian officers in the house behind ours and we soon became friendly with them. They would disappear for a few days on 'exercises' and return to Selsey with food parcels, which they would share out to us. A friend of mine in Cheltenham, Sybil, arranged for my horse to come down to Selsey by train and I cycled to Chichester, which was the nearest railway station, some eight miles away, to collect her.

I helped on a farm at Church Norton but was pretty awful at ploughing, so decided that the Land Army was not for me. Still not old enough to join up, I looked after Miss Scrimgeor's stables, as Paddy went to look after Lady Yules's valuable Arab horses.

At last, in November 1942, I was old enough to join up and I filled in an application form in the *Daily Express* and sent it off. My mother nearly had a fit when I told her what I had done and she said she hoped nothing would come of it. However, I received a letter telling me to report to Portsmouth for an interview, and having never been on a train by myself before, my mother insisted on coming with me, which didn't please me very much! The interview is a bit hazy to me now, but I remember filling in some squares and triangles; filling in more forms and being asked various questions by a WAAF officer. When asked what I would like to do in the WAAF I had no idea but when she discovered I could ride a horse and a bicycle, she suggested I become an MT driver. This sounded great, except that I knew nothing about cars, of course. Naturally I was very excited at the idea of becoming a military driver but my mother, as usual, said that nothing would come of it.

We now knew the war was really in progress, as there were many dog-fights in the sky over the sea. There were at least three airfields near us, the most active being RAF Tangmere. We were not many miles from Portsmouth, but of course all this activity increased my enthusiasm for joining the service and at last the day arrived when I received a letter telling me to report to RAF Innsworth in Gloucestershire on 1 January 1943. The next few weeks were spent saying my farewells and making arrangements for the horses to be looked after — I had acquired another horse on loan by then — and also had to get someone to look after Miss Scrimgeor's stables.

Christmas was spent at the usual parties and in addition we now had the Canadians to entertain; it was all great fun and added to my mother's misery, as they said I was far too young to join up.

2

JOINING UP AND TRAINING

1 January 1943

The great day arrived when I got on the train at Chichester by myself and said goodbye to my mother, telling her that I would take a taxi at Gloucester and that she need not worry because they knew I was coming! Little did I know what was ahead. After a good journey, I arrived at Gloucester with two other girls I had met on the train, who were also joining up, but we were shaken out of our composure when we saw what seemed to be hundreds of other girls arriving at the station yard amidst NCOs and lorries parking all over the place. We arrived at the camp in the dark, cold and snow. Once inside, we were issued with various pieces of equipment including a 'groundsheet' which indicated to us that we might be sleeping in tents! In fact these things were capes to put on in wet weather but were very awkward to wear. We were given medicals inclusive of FFI (free from infection) and our hair was examined for nits and other embarrassing examinations were carried out; some girls were marched away in another direction! We were then given a meal in the cookhouse — some concoction of kidneys floating in grey gravy which we tried to eat with our newly issued 'irons' — knife, fork and spoon — along with a tin mug. We were told to wash these utensils in a trough which was full of dirty bubbling water! At about midnight we were given some blankets and taken to our sleeping quarters. There were about thirty five of us to a hut and the beds did not have mattresses but three square things called 'biscuits'. There was plenty of moaning as we tried to get comfortable, being frozen stiff, and tried to keep the 'biscuits' from slipping away from each other!

The ablutions seemed to be miles away from the huts and there were no plugs in the baths but a hanky wound around a penny did the trick of stopping the water from running away. My fluffy bedroom slippers and quilted dressing gown soon became a mess in the snow and slush!

The next morning, when it was still dark, we were awoken by a tannoy announcing 'Wakey Wakey!' And so we had to vacate our beds smartish and be shown how to stack them away by the corporal in charge of the hut. Sheets and blankets had to be neatly folded and stacked into a 'sandwich' and then placed at the head of the bed. We were also shown how to polish our bedspace, the space on the left hand side of each bed, which was covered with the standard dark-brown 'ministry' lino that showed every mark! We then had breakfast in the cookhouse. This meal was better than that of the night before, although we could still have the grey-looking kidneys and gravy. We then spent the whole day marching here and there, sometimes for no reason at all, but we did have some intelligence examinations and other tests. By this time most of us had made friends with a particular girl we liked but it was difficult to keep together as we were shuttled around from pillar to post. My hopes of popping over to Cheltenham, only eight miles away, seemed to be impossible; in fact I never found the camp gates the whole week we were there!

The next few days we seemed to be in a daze of rushing here and there for more tests and the great kitting out of uniform. However, our excitement at being issued our uniforms was short-lived and we could not believe how awful the clothes looked on us none of them fitted. Perhaps they thought we would grow into them! The smart girl on the recruiting poster that said 'Serve in the WAAF with the men that fly' looked about one hundred per cent better than we shapeless beings! We were issued with white sausage-shaped bags which were called

27

'kitbags'. These we filled with various forms of clothing, including two different types of knickers, one light blue wool pair and one dark blue pair. Known as 'blackouts' and 'twilights' they came down to our knees. The pink cotton brassieres looked like jelly bags and certainly did not fit me so I didn't wear them. The striped pyjamas in flannelette also looked awful. We were warned that we must look after all the kit as we would be having kit-inspection on domestic nights when we had to lay out everything in a special way; this included a small white folding bag which was called a 'house-wife' because it contained sewing things, etc. The food had not improved but now we had discovered the NAAFI, where we could buy 'wads' — cakes — and cups of awful tea.

After a week at Innsworth we volunteers were given the option of returning home if we did not want to continue in the WAAF. Quite a few girls left but nothing on earth would induce me to leave, as I knew how pleased my mother would be to say to me, 'I knew you wouldn't like it'. At the end of that week, we were told that we would be leaving for our 'square-bashing' destination which turned out to be Morecambe, although we didn't know that at the time. On 8 January we were awakened at about 3.30 a.m., given breakfast and taken in lorries to Gloucester railway station, where we had to stand in alphabetical order for quite some time before the train arrived. As there were about 600 of us we were rather squashed up in the carriages with our kitbags, tin helmets and gas masks. I had tried wearing my gas mask but nearly suffocated, so I decided it would be more pleasant to be gassed! We finally arrived at Morecambe at 4.30 p.m. in the dark, and of course there were no names on the railway stations in those days.

Morecambe didn't mean much to me but I had a vague idea that it was a holiday resort in the north-west of the country. We were once again placed in alphabetical order and marched to our different billets, which turned out to be boarding houses managed by the famous 'landladies' of the north! I had made friends with a girl called Norma but she was allocated another billet and they wouldn't let anyone swap with another girl, so we could not be together. It turned out that my billet was quite

28

a nice house situated on the seafront with a kindly landlady. There were twelve of us to each house, three per room, and she looked after us very well, giving us eggs and bacon whenever possible.

The next three weeks were spent square-bashing up and down the promenade, having injections and doing gym in our knickers in some large dance hall which had been requisitioned by the RAF. I was soon in trouble over the length of my hair and had to carefully tuck it up under my cap, which was better than having it cut short. Several of us were nearly put on charge for walking along the seafront with our caps off, eating fish and chips. I managed to meet a boy I knew in Selsey, called Johnny Harman, who was on a course with the army nearby and hoped he would be given a commission shortly. It seemed strange to see him in uniform rather than on the beach at Selsey. There was still plenty of entertainment in Morecambe. I can remember seeing the *Gondoliers* and the *Mikado* at the main theatre. Both were extremely good and the applause very loud, as most of us in the audience were raw recruits in the services. Walks on the sands in the bracing air helped us to sleep and eat well, although, of course, the food was limited because of the rationing. The final passing-out parade arrived with the commanding officer's inspection. Ours' was the best turned out, which surprised most of us as we felt that our marching was somewhat erratic. Then we were given temporary postings to fill in time until we were called forward to start the MT course or whatever trade one was. Of the other two girls in my room Sally Davis was put on general duties and a Welsh girl became a batwoman.

On 29 January my posting came through for RAF Pocklington in Yorkshire, with eight other girls; sadly, my friend Norma was posted elsewhere and that was the end of my first friendship in the WAAF. Although we said we would write we did not get round to it.

RAF Pocklington — Yorkshire

After a long train journey the nine of us arrived at Pocklington and, as usual, were met by lorries to take us on to the camp.

At first, it seemed to be very drab and spread out and the WAAF quarters miles away from the main camp. We soon discovered it was a top line bomber station with Halifax aircraft of No. 102 Squadron. We thought it was very exciting and looked forward to seeing the planes take off on missions. Of course, as we were only U/T MT drivers, we were not allowed to drive and so had very little to do with the operational side of the station. The MT sergeant was forever telling us to go and clean some vehicle in order to get us out of his way! Our newly issued shoes did not help us very much when we had to walk nearly two miles to our billets so I asked my mother to send my bicycle up by train. It duly arrived at the LNER Station and made life much easier. When not cleaning out lorries I was able to explore some of the countryside around the airfield with some of the other girls who had bikes and, being early spring, we were able to pick primroses and snowdrops.

It wasn't long before I made friends with an American who had volunteered for aircrew duties in the RAF and we used to go to the Feathers Hotel with lots of others from the camp in Pocklington town. It was the first pub that I had ever been in and no doubt my mother would have had her usual fit if she had known. There were also shows on the camp by a theatre group, consisting of volunteers from the service personnel, and I remember a particularly attractive WAAF officer in one show, dancing with lots of chiffon around her to the tune of *Rhapsody in Blue*.

At the time Pocklington was heavily engaged in bombing Germany and most take-offs were at night and the return flights often ocurred about dawn. Many of the aircraft were shot up and as a result some very dicey landings, as the airmen called them, occurred. One of the MT girls was engaged to a pilot and he and his crew did not return one night; it was a very sad time for her and difficult for us to know how to comfort her. Arthur, the American, wasn't very pleased when a RAF pilot called Hugh started to chat me up in the Feathers Hotel one evening. He was a new pilot who had a brand new crew, very young and keen to get on Operations.

Then the sergeant decided to send us on leave to get us out

of the way. It was my first leave since joining up and I was looking forward to showing those at home my uniform, although I must say it didn't make me look very glamorous. I had the usual slow wartime journey down to London and then had to get across to Victoria to catch the Portsmouth train. I was sitting in a carriage at Victoria with a married couple whose son was in the RAF and they had just seen him off to his new station. In the course of our conversation it seemed that I would arrive at Chichester too late to catch a bus or taxi to Selsey so I would have to walk the eight miles in the dark. They suggested that I should stop the night with them at Croydon and continue the next day, and I readily accepted. It may seem silly these days but there were few cars on the roads and not a lot of houses had telephones. I shall forever be grateful to this kind couple for the good night's sleep, hearty breakfast and escort to the railway station to ensure that I got on the right train to Chichester. When I thanked them profusely they said that they hoped someone would do the same for their son should he get into similar difficulties. Such was the kindness and goodwill of the majority of people during the war years.

The week's leave went very quickly, catching up with some sleep, and seeing old friends and the horses again. On arriving back at the camp there was very little for us to do and the dates for the MT course had not come through yet, so it was decided to send us on leave again. Again, I arrived at Chichester too late to catch a bus or other means of transport. When I decided to walk to Selsey an airman who had been in the same carriage insisted on walking with me, as he thought it would be unsafe for me to do it on my own — today one would have thought the opposite — but at the time there was an air-raid on. As we were walking, we could hear the the planes and bombs in the Portsmouth area and every so often we had to dive into a ditch as a plane got nearer. We arrived at my mother's rather exhausted but after some tea and biscuits my mother lent her bicycle to the airman who said he would return it the next day. He was stationed at RAF Tangmere and he hadn't returned the bike by the time I had returned to the camp. However, a few days after my leave finished, he turned up at Selsey with

31

the bicycle and apologised to my mother for the time delay which had been caused by his being put on a week's 'jankers' for returning late to the camp the night he accompanied me home! It was a good deed on his part and I often wondered if my mother gave him the bus fare to get back to camp. Of course, the remarks at home were, 'What! you on leave again?' But I thoroughly enjoyed the various activities like riding my horse again and having a comfortable bed.

One of the Canadians, called Jack, who used to come to tea with us, wanted to see Scotland and was going on leave the same day as I was returning to camp. So he escorted me as far as York, after we had seen the sights of London such as Buckingham Palace, Trafalgar Square and other landmarks. There was no transport at York to the camp, due to the train being late, so we had to spend the night on the station and a very cold night it was too. The Canadians had all left Selsey by the time I had my next leave so I never saw any of them again.

The next few weeks went rather more quickly as we were allowed to accompany the drivers on their runs outside the camp to other airfields. Finally, at the end of March, our postings came through for us to go on the MT course. I left my bicycle with a girl called Milly and told her I would send for it when I knew my posting after the MT course, but I didn't send for it and my mother was furious. I visited Pocklington sometime later but my bike was not there, which was my own fault.

Hut 19.3. T.T. Wing RAF-Weeton

Whilst some of the girls had to wait for the course, I was very lucky and went on it straight away. Maybe this was due to the alphabetical system — my surname began with C. On 3 April I had a letter from one of the girls at Pocklington with the news that Hugh and his crew had been killed; they had been returning off Ops, shot up and injured, and crashed 500 yards from the end of the runway. They were all killed. I was shattered, of course, it being my first experience of this kind involving someone I knew and whose company I enjoyed. We had not even had time to write to each other as we had promised.

On the course we had BSM instructors and started with Austin 16 cars, two girls to each car, one driving and the other in the back. My friend Maureen was with me and she learnt very quickly, whilst I plodded along. We had driving lessons in the morning and theory in the afternoon, which I had great difficulty in absorbing. Gradually my driving improved but not the theory. Then we progressed to fifteen and thirty hundredweight lorries and on my eighteenth birthday I drove a three ton Albion lorry in convoy through the Mersey Tunnel. We also had night driving in convoys, going over the Pennines, and had to do handbrake change 'take-offs' on these steep slopes, which sometimes resulted in slipping backwards and getting dangerously near to the lorry behind. Of course we used to feel very important when we stopped at some café, dressed in uniforms with yellow leather gloves and leather jerkins over our battle dresses.

I managed to pass the practical tests but I'm sure that the examining sergeant on the theory side used to turn a 'Nelson's eye' to our written papers and pass them. Apart from the MT side we used to have GST (general services taining), such as mock invasions of the camps, usually at night when we were in bed, in order to get us out quickly and disperse the vehicles to safe places, previously designated. On 14 May we were sent on leave, having been given our various postings after passing the course. Maureen and I were posted to RAF Waterbeach near Cambridge and were to report there on 4 June 1943.

3

POSTINGS

RAF Waterbeach — Cambridgeshire

I met up with Maureen and Nicky, who had been on the same courses, at Liverpool Street Station and we arrived at Waterbeach late in the afternoon. We booked in and explored the station, which seemed well organised, and we were looking forward to staying there. But we were told that we would be part of a new unit called 1665 HCU (Heavy Conversion Unit) which would be leaving the next day for RAF Woolfox Lodge in Rutland near Stamford.

5 June RAF Woolfox Lodge, Stirling Aircraft

When we arrived at the airfield we soon discovered that it was a wartime station situated very near to the Great North Road, now the A1. This divided the domestic site from the airfield on the eastern side of the WAAF site, which was a long way from the MT section. It consisted of Nissen huts reached along a track which passed a lake and a lodge.

The nearest town was Stamford, a market town which has not changed very much except that the cinema has gone and there are more housing estates. There are some very pretty villages near Woolfox Lodge, such as Exton with its nice pub, the Fox and Hounds, adjacent to the village green. To reach it we used to cycle across the fields from our billets for some three miles along very bumpy tracks. I can remember one evening when we met a lot of aircrew boys at the pub who had walked there and they insisted on a lift back with us on our bikes. Needless to say, there were lots of spills and laughter on the journey back and the issued bikes suffered horribly. Whenever I see or have a ginger wine, I think of these times at the Fox and Hounds. I also remember the snow during the winter months which carpeted the whole countryside and made us feel really alive when we came off night-duty very early in the morning.

The MT section was pretty basic, consisting of two large bays in an old farmyard and a very cold rest room where we used to wait for our detail, whether it be on the camp or outside, or to collect and deliver crews to aircraft.

There was an officer in charge, a Sergeant Grayson and a Corporal Robinson, WAAF. We all enjoyed driving the crew coaches best, as this involved the sharp end of the war effort and was more appreciated by the aircrew! We also used to get the odd night-flying supper out of it if we took the crews extra distances to their billets instead of leaving them to walk across the Great North Road in the dark. The first time I was detailed to collect a crew from Stamford railway station, which was also my first run off the camp by myself, I was given the dreaded thirty hundredweight Fordson, which had no syncromesh gears. Each vehicle seemed to need different amounts of revs between gear changes and on this one I found I could not change down after having reached top. I arrived at Stamford station without mishap, there being no other traffic, but I was a bit worried about the return journey. To my horror I saw that I had parked the lorry in such a position that I had to reverse out. There was no way I could engage reverse gear, so I had to put my pride in my pocket and ask the crew I had come to collect to push the lorry round to the right direction, which did not exactly inspire their confidence in me. However, after such remarks from the pilot as I 'shouldn't be let loose on poor aircrew,' we arrived safely back at Woolfox Lodge in top gear!

The mechanics in the hangars always knew if we were new

from the course and they used to take the mickey out of us when we were on 'Maintenances' which meant we were there to fetch and collect gear all over the technical site. My first experience of this was when an airman seriously asked me to go to the store and collect a 'sky-hook', which I did, and it caused great amusement amongst the stores airmen.

One of our girls was on duty at station headquarters when a Stirling swung off the runway and carried on over the grass towards SHQ; she managed to get away but could not save the van and the aircraft demolished part of the building. It was a wonder they didn't have more accidents like this one as Stirlings were very prone to swinging at take-off and landing. We found night driving particularly hazardous, due to the masking of our headlights and the deceptive sounds on the dispersal areas between aircraft running up the engines and actually taxi-ing so we did have some near misses and one or two accidents. I was waiting on the peritrack for a plane to land one day when it swung on landing. By revving like mad I managed to avoid being badly damaged by backing my vehicle as fast as possible.

When I was on duty, driving the signals van out to the aircraft, I used to like climbing into them to explore them while waiting for an order to go to stores or fetch another mechanic. On one occasion, when I was in the aircraft, a corporal told me to go to the back and blow down some tubes on the side of the fuselage. I often wondered why the corporal thought it was so funny when I returned to the front to tell him that I had done as he asked me to do. Many years later, when telling my husband about this, he roared with laughter and told me the tubes were there for the airmen to 'spend a penny' in flight when they were taken short!

I had a nasty experience when driving a fifteen hundredweight van on the airfield. The van was filled with ammunition, which suddenly started to explode in the back of the vehicle. I stopped the van almost at the same time as I bailed out one side, while the airman armourer jumped out of the other side. The van finally stopped on the grass with the ammunition still exploding. Apparently it was bad loading that had caused the ammunition to explode. Luckily, it had only been practice material.

What a 'Bloomer'! 303 good reasons for 'Ammo' truck bale-out

We were always keen to get outside runs off the camp and many of these runs were to other bomber airfields, of which there were many in the Cambridge area. I did not enjoy one such run when the fog descended, as it often did in the Fenlands. This time it turned into thick fog — so much so that I had to vacate my vehicle to find some kind of landmark. After a bit of searching I couldn't find the vehicle again and had to wait for the fog to clear. Luckily there was no other traffic in the area.

Names of girls I can remember in the MT section include: Maureen, Nicky and Joyce, Spud, Margaret, Ann, Steve, but there were some others whose names escape me now. One of the girls called Red, was very attractive and always looked immaculate. She became friends with the pilot of a Canadian crew and I with his observer, called Vernon. He was very generous and shared his food parcels from home with me, when I was in my lorry on duty outside Flying Control, waiting to pick up crews. The crew were posted to Downham Market and the last time I saw Vernon was when he waved to me from a Stirling taxi-ing around the peritrack at Woolfox Lodge.

At a disadVANtage in foggy Cambridgeshire!

We wrote to each other for a time and then lost touch. Red married the pilot but, sadly, he was shot down shortly afterwards on Operations and later was a POW Vernon was not on that operation, due to a heavy cold, and was grounded. He later went on to 7 Squadron Path Finders on Lancasters.

In October, I collected a mainly Australian crew from Stamford railway station and became friends with the pilot, who was called Ron. He was very charming and had practically no Aussie accent. I used to go out with him and his crew when they were not night flying and on the last evening of their course we all went to the pub on the Great North Road, called the Ram-Jam, and had a very jolly time. The next day I drove them to the station and we were made to kiss goodbye whilst the crew took photographs which probably never came out. They were posted to Tarrant Rushton, 196 Squadron. Ron wrote to me for a few months.

Another sadness: Maureen had a letter from home saying that her brother had been killed in Sicily, so she had to go on leave to comfort her parents. I had previously spent a forty-eight-hour pass with Maureen at her home. Nicky also asked me to her home on another forty-eight-hour pass and we managed to get a lift on the back of an open lorry. You can imagine that we were so cold on arriving on the outskirts of London that we could hardly walk! We got the tube to Brentwood where Nicky lived and we had a nice break. It was so difficult to get to Selsey for short periods.

Woolfox Lodge was a sea of mud and we were forever getting stuck with our vehicles and losing wellies, but at Christmas we were allowed to wear civilian clothes for the various camp entertainments. There were a lot of Americans in Stamford and of course they used to chat us up. Maureen rather liked one called Clyde and he had a friend called Coffee; why I cannot remember except that he was not dark. However I was not keen on the Yanks and never went to their camp dances, which they arranged on a grand scale, sending transport for the girls at Woolfox Lodge. On one occasion, when a number of Fortresses were diverted to us, I was detailed to pick up some of the crews from the dispersal areas and I couldn't resist saying to them how small their aircraft looked compared to the Stirling! However, they took it in good humour, remarking that it didn't look like a Short Stirling — the maker's name.

4

RAF TILSTOCK

20 January

As the MT was part of the 1665 HCU we moved with them to RAF Tilstock and Maureen, Spud, Rennee and I drove the de-icer lorries there and returned on the coach. On the 21st we finally departed, driving more lorries to Tilstock. Both journeys were uneventful but we were sorry to leave Woolfox Lodge in spite of the bad ground conditions there. There was already a unit, 81 OTU at Tilstock, which had Whitley aircraft and an established MT section. The MT personnel, I think, at first resented us intruding but after a while we settled in well. The MT officer was Flight Lieutenant Burne who had a WAAF Sergeant Porter in charge of the WAAFs and two WAAF corporals. Sergeant Porter avoided doing any driving herself and landed us new girls with all the dirty jobs, such as the coal run, which was done with a horrid little Bantam lorry and a very cheeky crew of 'coal-wallahs'. We were also put on sanitation vehicles which were loaded by the Italian POW's and of course we had to do the water — bowser run. None of these were popular details, as you can imagine. However, having proved our worth, Sergeant Porter began to give us more interesting runs and we felt we were really a part of the section at last. After we had been given familiarisation on the local countryside and other units, we were able to go onto a twenty-four-hour shift system on the crew coach.

Stirlings and Silver Birches
1665 HCU Tilstock 1944.

We had, by now, discovered the local pubs and cafés near the airfield: the Raven and the Witchbowl Hotel, a café called Dirty Lils, which was the best place to have egg and chips and another café near the camp, called the College, where we used to go after night duty. Being a wartime camp the main road ran through the airfield but it had been closed for the duration. We were first billeted in the dreaded Nissen huts, which were always damp, but soon moved to some better, and drier, accommodation on the main site, called Laing huts. Whitchurch was our nearest town, some three miles away; not very lively but it had a cinema and a decent hairdresser's which I soon visited.

One of the crew coaches was a left hand drive Dodge, the other a Fordson, in which we waited to pick up crews outside the crew room to transport them from and to dispersals and squadron crew rooms. Many a letter was written home whilst we were waiting. I remember Marjorie used to write to her fiancé every day when she was on duty. He was in the army, stationed in India.

A Stirling overshot the end of the runway one day and ended up straddled across the main road, but luckily no traffic was moving in the vicinity. And one night another Stirling overshot in the dark and taxied along the road back onto the peritrack of the airfield. The next day we saw the tyre marks to prove it! Gliders arrived in March 1944, which meant we had to keep a special eye out for the towing cable when they were released from the aircraft. Sadly, one glider crew was killed when they hit some wires soon after they became airborne from the airfield.

I was now going on more interesting runs further away. One was to Worksop near Nottingham. Ginger Dutton usually did this run but she was on leave so I was detailed to do it and had an airmen to help me collect the oxygen cylinders. I had a fifteen hundredweight Bedford. On our return trip the airmen persuaded me to do a slight detour so that he could see his wife who was expecting a baby shortly. We stayed longer than we should have and it was getting dark. Much to my horror, the lorry started pinking and the weather was worsening with heavy snow falling. The wipers did not work properly and in the end

43

I had to stop. We decided we had better stay put until light or the weather improved. We had a very cold night and the snow kept falling. The windows let some of it in as they were the plastic type with side flaps. The morning seemed an eternity away but when it did arrive and we managed to get out of the lorry and made our way up the road as best we could, we found we were only about a hundred yards from a pub! If only we had known we might have had a more comfortable night. We had breakfast there and, with shovels, dug the lorry out and managed to get it going again. We eventually arrived back at camp where there was some explaining to do! Luckily I never had to do that run again.

Another incident, at Tilstock, involved a run I had near Derby. I can't remember why, but I was on my own, and on my return decided I would have a look at Derby. I parked my lorry in one of the bomb site car parks and wandered into the shopping area. Unfortunately, I had not noted where the car park was and when I tried to find it I couldn't. In great panic and almost in tears, I managed to find a policeman and we eventually found my lorry.

Another trip we had was to Hawkstone Priory which was a training place for Roman Catholic priests. We used to bring them to camp so they could take communion there. However, this trip it was snowing when I left camp and as I got nearer Hawkstone it became really bad and, again with wiper trouble, I got out of my van to see if I could find the entrance. The blizzard was getting worse. I managed to find the door and after much banging, it opened. I was taken into a large hall with a log fire burning, given some hot cocoa and biscuits and dried off a bit. When the blizzard eased off we went to find my van and with shovels again cleared a way until I found the road and returned to camp minus the priest it was too late for him then!

When we were on the Beam Approach Run which was at Fenns Moss (some airmen were on shifts there and we had to fetch them when they changed over), we usually called in at a pub called the Waggoners.

Our satellite station was Sleap and to reach it we had to drive through Wem, which was full of black American troops. They used to sit on a wall and make catcalls at us when they were off duty. I can remember one of them had auburn hair.

Our social life was quite busy as the aircrews did not fly all the time, although they had lectures when not doing so. Graham and his friend Andy, Beryl and I used to make up a four and had some good times together. One evening we were all coming back from the village of Prees and a pub called the Harp when we were stopped by a local bobby who took our names and service numbers, as we had no lights on our bicycles. Graham and Andy were most upset and asked the policeman to forget it, there being a war on, but he refused. So we were each fined about 7s.6d. nearly three days' pay to me! The boys were posted at the end of the course to 620 Squadron at Fairford, Gloucester and Graham wrote to me for a time but we lost touch and I wonder if he survived the war. One day I hitched into Chester with Freddy, who was on the staff, to see a concert by the Liverpool Philharmonic Orchestra, conducted by Malcolm Sargent. I thought this rather dull and I asked Freddy why there weren't any pianos; he was horrified at my ignorance.

Maureen, who was going out with a Corporal Ron Brown*, was posted to Tarrant Ruston. She asked me if I would swap with her for this posting so that they could stay together but I didn't want to leave all my friends in 1665 HCU. I felt rather guilty in refusing her but subsequently received an invitation to their wedding which, unfortunately, I was unable to attend as I could not get my duty changed. Taffy, after a very brief courtship, married an airman called Johnny who she first met in the dark when cycling back to the camp one evening! We all rallied round to contribute as much clothing and presents as wartime coupons and rationing would allow.

On 3 May I was nineteen years' old and had a party in the section. Nicky's mother made a lovely cake with pink and white icing, which arrived in the post undamaged — it was amazing

---

* After the war Ron, the brother of Lord George Brown, was a labour M.P.

Pilot Error ... 'Stop me and buy one!'

how the postal services kept going so well — and we had quite a peacetime binge with it and other food and drink which the girls had saved up.

One of the more hazardous airfield duties was driving the 'Stop — Follow Me' standard van which was mainly used for visiting aircraft, to guide them from the runway to their allotted dispersals. There was an illuminated board on the back of the van with the two words written facing rearwards and operated from the cab of the vehicle by the driver. On one occasion Pat Kelly put out her stop light when approaching an intersection to the peritrack but the aeroplane didn't stop and went into the back of her van; she managed to jump out before more damage was done and was unhurt, but very shaken. We were quite close to our satellite relief airfield, Sleap near Wem, which was used by Whitley aircraft and CT (continuation training). During night-flying circuits and bumps, an aircraft swung off the runway and hit the flarepath hut close to the control tower, killing two WAAF drivers who were on duty inside.

I had a short spell driving the ambulance when the usual

driver, Pat, was on leave. I didn't like the duty very much, especially when I had to attend an aircraft crash near Oswestry involving a Mosquito from another station. The Mosquito had gone straight into the ground, killing a young pilot on his twenty first birthday.

A none too popular duty was when we were detailed to make a night-time trip in a lorry, usually a thirty hundredweight Fordson, with some aircrew and airmen, to a field which seemed to be in the middle of nowhere, and sit and wait for containers to be dropped by Stirlings. It usually entailed driving over muddy fields trying to find the containers which wasn't easy. Little did we know how important this exercise was until Arnhem happened later on. At the time it just seemed a waste of time to sit in freezing conditions in our lorries for most of the night!

My mother wrote to me on 8 May, advising me that the air raids were getting worse in Selsey and that she had rented a cottage at Symonds Yat in Herefordshire, after a piece from an aircraft had crashed through the thatched roof of the house she was living in. She arranged for a farmer to look after my horses and I managed to get some leave and visit her at the cottage which was situated in lovely countryside in the Wye Valley.

During the end of May and early June we had many outside runs to bomber airfields when the aircrew had finished their conversion course. I'll never forget one hazardous trip when I had to take crews to RAF Fairford, it was like a shuttle run service replacing crews. Johnny, the RAF driver, drove the crew coach and I drove the dreaded thirty hundredweight lorry with the baggage, and had a very nice young aircrew chap as my passenger. I had been keen to get on with the run as I hoped to see Graham and Andy, who had been posted to this particular station. However, they were not around and Johnny and I started off on our return trip; the first thing that happened was that the canvas became loose on the back of the lorry and blew over the front of my driving cab but luckily Johnny had seen it happen and rescued me. Within fifty miles of camp, my lorry started to make awful noises in the engine and after inspection, I found that it had run out of oil! I'd done my DI before leaving

Tilstock but not before leaving Fairford because I thought it would be all right for the return journey. We removed the rope from the canvas and used it as a tow rope. When I tried to switch the lights on as it was getting dark they didn't work which made things worse as I couldn't see in front of me at all. It was a nasty feeling and took us a long time but we had to carry on as the crew coach was needed the next morning for another trip to Fairford. We arrived back at the MT yard in the small hours of the morning. I was dreading the next day as I had to put a note on the F 658 stating that the lorry was unserviceable and why. Luckily I was not put on a charge as everyone was too busy to bother with things like that at that time. I learnt my lesson and from then on always made a double check when I did a DI.

I was now a Leading Aircraftwoman, having passed my theory and driving test. I was making many more runs to other RAF stations as I was now one of the more experienced drivers. One such run that stands out in my memory was when I was taking four Canadian officers to Netheravon in Wiltshire; as we approached the camp one of the back wheels came off and we slithered into the ditch, rather gracefully as it happened!

The Canadians were shaken but unhurt and very critical of the WAAF drivers until they realised it wasn't my fault. The MT section, in fact, were able to repair the vehicle for the return journey the next day.

One of the funniest memories I have of Tilstock was of a white bull terrier called Sinbad, who, I think, belonged to a Wing Commander. Sinbad used to join the bus queue to Whitchurch in the evenings, unaccompanied, get on the bus and usually onto a seat and woe betide anyone who tried to get him off! No one found out where he went or why, although we suspected he had a few lady friends in the town! He certainly had many scars to prove his worth. He was always in the bus queue for the return trip to camp!

It was also rumoured that there was some kind of ghost on the far side of the airfield. The only experience I had of this was when I was driving in the dark around the peritrack on the far side. Suddenly my lights faded and the ignition cut out for a second or so. It was an eerie feeling and I drove back to the MT section straight away to have the electrical system checked, but there was nothing wrong with it. I heard some time later that some of the other girls had a similar experience, although I never mentioned mine to them, nor had anyone else before.

Beryl and I hitched to Manchester when on a stand-down and were picked up by the SP's for wearing brown gloves when in uniform — terrible! We were given a dressing down by our WAAF commanding officer, Mrs Cunningham-Watson.

Apart from some ENSA shows on the camp such as Elfredo and his band on concert, nothing much happened at this time. I went on leave to see my mother who had moved once again, to Rose Cottage at Hewellsfield, still in the Wye Valley; very quaint with an outside loo! Whilst I was on leave my grandmother had a stroke and I had to have my leave extended, as my mother couldn't cope with the situation on her own. I finally returned to camp on 20 December. We had Christmas on the camp which turned out to be very good; we had an excellent Christmas dinner in the mess with all the trimmings and we went to see *This is the Army* at the camp cinema later on in the day. We saw 1945 in on New Year's Eve at the dance at the sergeants' mess where I saw Jimmy, an old friend, again. He had been at Woolfox and had just been commissioned. He had completed his second tour on Stirlings and was posted to Sleap for special duties, something hush-hush. The next day we went to Whitchurch to the cinema and saw *Gone with the Wind*. We missed the last bus back to camp and got soaking wet in the rain.

February brought thick snow and ice with icicles hanging from the billet roof eaves. With no water in ablutions, the icicles came in very useful for melting down in the kettle for making tea and washing.

It was so cold that we lived with our thick issue pyjamas — which we had all hated when we first saw them at Innsworth — under our battle dresses. The worst part was starting the lorries from cold in the early mornings and trying to get the ice off.

When the weather was better I went on a weekend pass to

Christmas Day, 1944
Menu.

BREAKFAST (09.00):
WHEATFLAKES and MILK
FRIED EGG   GRILLED BACON
MARMALADE
BREAD   BUTTER
TEA and COFFEE   BREAKFAST ROLLS.

DINNER (12.30):
THICK MOCK TURTLE SOUP
ROAST TURKEY   STUFFING
CHIPALATA SAUSAGE
ROAST PORK   APPLE SAUCE
BRUSSEL SPROUTS   PEAS IN BUTTER
ROAST and MASHED POTATOES
XMAS PUDDING   BRANDY SAUCE
MINCE PIE   CUSTARD
DESSERT
BEER,   MINERALS,   CIGARETTES

TEA (16.30):
COLD BOILED HAM   HOME-MADE PICKLES
SAUCE
BREAD and BUTTER
XMAS CAKE   PRESERVES   TEA.

SUPPER (from 21.00):
COLD MEATS,   SALADS,   PICKLES
BREAD   COFFEE and COCOA

THE STATION COMMANDER
AND
OFFICERS WISH YOU ALL

A HAPPY CHRISTMAS

ROYAL AIR FORCE STATIONS
TILSTOCK & SLEAP

A Merry Christmas
and
A Happy New Year

25th DECEMBER, 1944.

R.A.F. OR WORKS UNIT STAMP :

ROYAL AIR FORCE. *Unit Serial No.....................*

R.A.F. Form 658.

Application for Mechanical Transport for Duty Journey

PART 1—To be filled in by applicant.

1. Reason for not using public conveyance....... *None available* ....
   (This <u>must</u> be filled in by the applicant and the reason stated concisely, e.g., "None available"
   or "<u>saving of time essential</u>" or "operational necessity," etc. Abbreviations are not to be
   used, nor are the words "EXPEDIENCY" or "CONVENIENCE."

2. Nature of Duty (in full)....... *Returning to Sleap after C.M.*

3. Passengers or load for which transport is required *7/12 Main Guard*

4. From....... *O/c — Mess* *To .... *Sleap*
   ⁂ (State all places at which)
   (duty calls are to be made)

5. Date ... *28/9/44* .... Time of Pick·Up ... *1400*

6. Place of pick-up or at which to report......... *Officers Mess.*

7. Approximate length of time for which required......... *1 hr.*

8. A load <u>has not</u> been arranged for the reverse journey ....
   * ~~has~~

9. Passengers <u>will not</u> use the car on reverse journey ....
   * ~~will~~

   * Strike out if not applicable.

   Time and Date *1200 — 28/9/44* hours.   Signature ... *J.K. Grant*

   Wt.11961/O182 5,000M. 5/44 W.E.&3. 51-9297

Above: An application for transport. The guardroom joke when we had a run
to Sleap with officers again.
Left: The Christmas Menu 1944.

Beryl's home in Leintwardine in Shropshire. It was a pretty village and her parents lived in a very attractive beamed cottage. Beryl lent me some of her civilian clothes so we managed to go out and about locally without causing too much attention.

Back at the station in March, Anne and I were duty drivers on standby when we were wakened by the duty NCO telling us that they were expecting 160 aircrew. They were being diverted to Tilstock because they couldn't land at their own airfield, due to German fighters attacking them in their own circuit. In fact two Stirlings had already been shot down. However, the rest landed safely with us and we took them to de-briefing and ferried quantities of tea and refreshments for them in the crew rooms. They all looked very tired and dejected as their squadron had had a bad time of it in the last few days.

5

MORE AIRFIELDS

26 March 1945 — RAF Saltby Leicestershire

We were on the move again. 1665 HCU was moving to RAF
Saltby in Leicestershire, another wartime airfield out in the
sticks. I drove some officers there in a staff car and they all had
a bit of a shock when we approached the rather drab and bleak
airfield in the depths of the country.

The camp was very spread out, and involved much walking
in the mud, which we were used to by now. The HCU now
had Halifax aircraft as well. There were two villages fairly near,
Thruxton about three miles from camp and Saltby about a mile
from the far side of the airfield, which had a pub called the *Nag's
Head*, very popular among the aircrew. Grantham was about
nine miles away and although we could catch a bus into the town
we often had to get a taxi back, which wasn't so bad if there
were enough of us to share the cost — £1 in those days was a
lot. I was a little worried when an aircrew chap I knew asked
me to go to his home on leave, but I did go and got on very
well with his parents at their house in Surrey. His father had
a car and let Bob drive us around using the precious petrol
coupons which were very scarce in those days. We had some
nice drives around the area. Later on I went with him to his
home again, which coincided with my twentieth birthday, and
his married sister made me a cake. We also had a day out in
London, where you could still get a good meal if you were willing

to pay for it.

If we wanted enough time off to make it worthwhile to go away off the camp, we used to do a double shift in the crew coach duty. That would give us forty eight hours off after the duty finished and the NCOs used to turn a blind eye to this arrangement. I suspect they did the same kind of thing themselves. However, we used to get over tired which was rather a silly thing to do when one had to drive large vehicles and valuable aircrew around.

On 7 May there was great excitement on the camp as the word spread around that the war in Europe was finished. At first we found it hard to believe, as we were in bed at the time after a long shift.

Some of the girls went down to the sergeants' mess where a boisterous party was in the making and, as a result there were a lot of thick heads in the morning. The next evening Chris and I went to York to celebrate and found the whole city had gone mad with brass bands playing, fireworks going off and dancing in the streets.

On 29 May, whilst night-flying was in progress, a Stirling swung on take-off and collided with a line of parked C-46's in a dispersal area. I was waiting at the end of the runway in my lorry and watched, horrified, as it hit the first aircraft and burst into flames killing an American airman who was asleep in it. The crew of the Stirling were all right apart from cuts and burns.

I had become friendly with a local farmer when visiting the Nags Head in Saltby and in the course of conversation we talked about horses. He said he had a nice horse which needed exercising and asked if I would like to ride it. I was very pleased to be able to ride again and readily accepted. The horse was a lovely Hunter which hadn't been ridden for a year but he didn't tell me he had been feeding it oats all that time! I had an exhausting ride but managed to stay on despite the mare galloping like the wind. The farmer seemed surprised to see me still on top when I returned to his yard and said as the horse had been useless in the hunting field, I could keep her! Of course I couldn't as it was impossible to have a horse on camp and I also knew we wouldn't be at Saltby very long.

Move to Marston Moor — 31 July 1945

On 31 July we were once again on the move, this time to Marston Moor in Yorkshire. It was a very good camp but as usual well dispersed and we were all issued with bikes. It was very hot for the first few weeks we were there and we managed to find somewhere to swim in the river nearby.

We had one serious accident on 9 October when a Stirling failed to maintain height and crashed into the village street of Tockworth; it hurtled along the rooftops for about half a mile, bouncing off different houses. About seventeen houses were hit or damaged before the aircraft broke up. It was a miracle that only one person was killed in the village and that was the village postman, Arthur Caskill. About twenty families were made homeless. All the crew were killed and all the village was left in total shock. The older residents still living there remember the dreadful accident to this day.

The war over, my mother decided to move back to Cheltenham but she had to rent accommodation as our house was still let for another year. On 6 August, 1945, the first atomic bomb was released over Japan, killing an estimated 70,000 Japanese and on the 8th another atomic bomb was dropped on Nagasaki. This finally broke all further resistance from the Japanese. They agreed to accept the unconditional terms of surrender, which was signed on 23 September and so World War Two ended. More celebrations, of course, although we wouldn't have been quite so pleased if we had realised what the horrific consequences of the bomb had been and indeed, the lasting effects of it.

On 7 November we moved to a pre-war station, Linton-on-Ouse, Yorkshire. It was a very smart station with mostly permanent buildings and many married quarters, of which some were vacant and had been allocated to WAAF personnel. What a luxury having a house with an inside toilet and bathroom and three bedrooms — two girls to each. I shared with Chris, Pat with Spud, Steve with Ann. On 13 November Steve went to York for some reason and came back with a mongrel dog called Biff and I said I would help look after him. He was great fun and no trouble at first. I went on leave to Cheltenham before Christmas and stayed over for the festivities and, although I enjoyed seeing my old friends, I missed the girls from the MT section. Of my old friends not many had joined the services but had been doing essential jobs in the police and the Red Cross and National Savings. Tony had joined the army and had had an argument with a tank which got the better of him. He was pretty ill in hospital for some time but I didn't know that at the time of my leave. When I arrived back at camp they told me that Biff had killed ten chickens, and a farmer on whose land Biff had been tresspassing had shot and grazed the dog. The police said that we must have Biff destroyed but neither Steve nor I could bring ourselves to do it and Ann said she would see that it was done. It was very sad as he was a nice little dog, but we couldn't risk keeping him.

The year 1946 started with a lot of ice and fog, so very little flying was possible. I met an aircrew chap at one of the camp dances who said that as he entered the room he saw a 'glow' around me and had fallen in love with me; I thought he was nuts and burst out laughing, much to his dismay. When I learnt that he had just returned from overseas I told him he had been in the sun too long. He took me out to dinner the next evening and asked me to marry him and go with him to Cairo where he had been offered a good job. Of course all this was too sudden and I did wonder if he found someone else with a 'glow' around her!

In April my mother wrote to me with the sad news that my horse Nimble had broken out of her field at Church Norton (near Selsey) and had been killed on a land mine on the shoreline there. Renny, my other horse, was all right but it was shattering news. I managed to get some leave for my twenty-first birthday in May and went down to Selsey where my mother had rented a house for a week so I arranged for some friends to look after Renny permanently.

While at camp I had been part of a foursome, with Alec, Steve and a sergeant called Vin. Alec and I hadn't realised Steve and Vin were seriously courting until they announced that they were going to get married in Newton Church, which was just outside

56

the camp boundary and invited Alec and I, and also Doug and Ann. They were married on a lovely summer's day in the church, which was very small but attractive. Steve wore a black costume and a black Juliet cap. Her parents didn't come to the wedding, not because of the black outfit, I might add! After the service we went to York and had lunch at Betty's. If you go to Betty's nowadays you can still see the signatures of many of the wartime aircrew on the mirrors in the downstairs lower dining room. We returned to camp, leaving them to have their forty-eight-hour honeymoon in York.

We had all moved into barrack blocks by now, which were quite comfortable but not as good as the married quarters. One day Chris and her boyfriend managed to hire a tandem and Alec and I went for a ride to Knaresborough for tea with them. It was a hilarious ride and we all had a go at riding the monster, which I did not like. That month I had a detail to Castle Howard, home of the Earl of Carlisle, but now some military establishment.

In July I had my first driving accident — in Yorkshire, after having dropped some officers off somewhere in a staff car I was driving. I was happily returning to camp on a clear summer's day and was turning right, with a blind corner to my left, when a car came round the corner on the wrong side and hit me broadside, spinning me round until I was facing the other way. I was very shaken and my wing mirror was ripped off and the door was badly dented. I had to fill in one of the accident forms which we always carried with us, showing the location of the crash and skid marks and so on on a drawing. On reporting back to the MT officer I was relieved to find that I wasn't put on a charge. After some consideration it was judged that the accident hadn't been my fault.

Whilst we were at Linton-on-Ouse, we were given a pep talk by a WAAF officer to the effect that we were not to wear each other's caps or share combs on any account; there had been an outbreak of nits amongst some of the girls — not amongst MT though! This gave me the stupid idea of walking across the parade ground from NAAFI towards SHQ carrying my hat and hoping that the WAAF officer might be looking out of her office window and see me. The reason I was confident on this point was because previously I had swopped hats with Pat Kelly, as she always seemed to make hers into a better shape than mine. My luck was in when the WAAF officer saw me and shouted out of her window, 'Airwoman, report to me immediately'. In I marched and explained why I wasn't wearing my hat: it wasn't mine and I had taken it by mistake and was on my way now to returning it to its rightful owner. So of course, she calmed down and allowed me to go without charge.

I know WAAF officers must have had a difficult time keeping control of us WAAFs and most of them were very considerate in their dealings with us. I remember an occasion at Tilstock when I was called on the tannoy to report to the WAAF CO. Naturally I thought that something very serious had happened but I was horrified to hear that my mother had rung up the CO to say that she had not heard from her daughter for two weeks! The WAAF CO was very kind and told me to write home immediately.

6

RAF DISHFORTH AND DEMOB

On 15 July 1946 1665 HCU was disbanded and some of it absorbed by 1332 HTCU at RAF Dishforth near Boroughbridge in Yorkshire. I was one of the drivers posted to 1332 HTCU, which was a Transport Command conversion unit converting crews mainly to York type aircraft, which were to fly out to the Middle and Far East as freight and passenger aircraft. Many of the girls were getting demobbed and it was suggested that some of us sign on, but I didn't like the idea, especially as my closer friends were leaving or not coming to Dishforth. Pat, Spud and Winnie were also posted with me so it wasn't too bad, but it was goodbye to our favourite aircraft, Stirlings and Halifaxes. Dishforth was a peacetime station and situated about three miles from Ripon, which was a very attractive market town where we could, for some reason, get real cream cakes in a café.

We girls were again put into the vacant airmen's married quarters, which were quite comfortable. I was put on the crew coaches which were Bedford Trooper types and easier to drive than the Fordsons.

At Dishforth they had German POWs still biding their time until they were returned to Germany. One I can remember was called Werner and was very good-loking. He had been shot down earlier in the war, and most of his family had been killed by bombs. We did not talk about it, though. When I was on duty with the control van, I used to sit in the flare path hut with the lads, and if I missed my breakfast, which was quite often, Werner used to fry some bread and put sugar on it (his version of a doughnut) and make me some cocoa; it always tasted very good. He had also adopted a mongrel bitch which had puppies; one of them he gave to me. My mother was not very pleased when I took the puppy home for her to look after. Unfortunately he had fits and she had to have him put to sleep. I did not tell Werner though. I don't know what happened to the POWs as they moved on somewhere else.

Alec was still at Linton-on-Ouse and we arranged to meet in York one evening. Whilst I was waiting for him at York railway station a car full of young RAF officers passed by and then came round again so that they could wave at me — I was in civilian clothes at the time. I did not think about the incident again until the next day when an officer who was a member of the crew waiting for my crew coach said to me, 'Didn't I see you at York Station yesterday afternoon?' I said I was there and he told me he had been driving the car full of his crew. His name was Peter and he asked me whether I would like to go out with him that evening.

We spent a few evenings together and liked each other's company. I went on leave to Cheltenham where he wrote to me. When I told him that my mother was giving me a car to drive back to camp he gave me some petrol coupons which were very scarce in those days of rationing. The car my mother gave me was a 1936 Vauxhall 14 Coupé which had quite a good engine but which got better after I had lent it to one of the MT mechanics who, for the use of the car, put some petrol in it although the petrol gauge didn't work. I could not understand why the car felt better after each time I lent it to him until I realised that the Commanding Officer's car was also a Vauxhall and he was now complaining that it wasn't running very well!

My romance with Peter was developing into a close relationship and we went to the Lake District on a stand-down to Windermere which was very quiet and lovely for walking and boating. We naturally saw a lot of each other whilst Peter was on the course; he flew with a very good pilot called Dicky who later became assistant commandant of the RAF College at Cranwell and then an Air Marshal. They were posted to Homsley South, a wartime airfield near Christchurch in Hampshire, for flying duties on Yorks on the route which involved transporting service personnel from the Middle and Far East after carrying supplies on the outbound legs.

Peter had completed his tour on Liberators on 86 Squadron at Tain in Scotland and had since been on the route with the same squadron at Oakington. The squadron had changed roles, from Coastal to Transport Command. He told me how lucky he had been to do his OTU at Nassau in the Bahamas before going to Dorval in Canada to fly on Temporary Transport, delivering Liberators to the UK. Also, he said, 'If I had been selected for Bomber Command, you probably wouldn't be putting up with me now!'

We had decided to get married and I spent a weekend at his family's home in Birmingham with his mother and stepfather, who was the senior medical officer of ICI Birmingham. Later I spent Christmas there and we went to a few parties given by his parent's friends.

After Christmas, when Peter was on the route, I was due to be demobbed and was one of the last of the original girls on 1665 HCU. Pat had gone home on demob, Spud had got married to Syd who was on the ground staff of the conversion unit, but to her horror she was still posted to Leeming before being demobbed. January was bitterly cold with a lot of snow on the airfield and we all had to do our bit on the snow-clearance plan. Then I was able to start clearing from the unit, as my demob was due. Having done all the necessary I had some of the girls to celebrate in my billet with cups of cocoa, which I brewed up on my old and trusted electric fire which I had had for several years. Suddenly, the duty WAAF officer came into the billet and saw the fire. 'Airwoman, what are you doing with that fire? It is strictly against regulations'. (This I knew.) 'Report at 0900 hours tomorrow morning at SHQ.' I was put on a charge, the first one during the whole four years of service, and I also got another rocket for having my hair too long, as if it

61

mattered at that stage. I knew the WAAF officer didn't like me, especially as I was going out with an aircrew officer, so I expected the worst, but not the punishment I received. The WAAF CO said that I would have my demob deferred for one month and that I would have to report to the guard room three times a day for a week. So I had to go round the station and book in at all the sections again.

Peter was out in India for most of that month so I didn't worry too much, except I didn't see the logic of keeping me in the service when I was doing very little for my keep. My mother, of course, was more disappointed than I. When I had my final interview with the CO, who seemed oblivious of my misdemeanor, he asked me if I had any comments of the service. I was about to say what I thought of the pettiness of the punishment I had just received after four years of a clean record, but thought better of it when I saw the WAAF officer standing in the background starting to bristle. Better play it cool than to get my demob further delayed. So I left Dishforth the next day and handed in my uniform at RAF Kirkham and walked out as a civilian once more. When I read the remarks in my service book, it read: 'LACW Cronk has been employed as an MT Driver for four years and has given every satisfaction as a driver and has had a very good service record characterwise. She is recommended for sectretarial work in civilian life.' It was dated 6 February 1947. I thought it rather amusing, as I couldn't type at all!

I would have liked to have kept my uniform; some of the girls had done so by saying that they had no civilian clothes to wear. I wonder what happened to all our uniforms. I expect they went on the bonfire, suffering a rather similar fate to the Stirling and Halifax aircraft later on; none were kept for future generations to see; they were completely destroyed. I will never forget the first time I saw a Halifax. It seemed huge until I saw a Stirling, which really was big!

I enjoyed my four years in the WAAF and have made some lifelong friends and found happiness with a husband I wouldn't have met but for the war. Such is fate. It is a pity war brings so much sadness to some and so much happiness to others.

Peter and I were married in July 1947 and Peter stayed in the Royal Air Force until 1969. Our son, who is married, is now also in the RAF.

7

R.C. BURNE — EX MT OFFICER, RAF TILSTOCK

Not many airmen have had the doubtful pleasure of sending themselves a telegram calling themselves up. This happened to me when I was training in the Auxiliary Air Force along with many more from the Manchester area in August 1939.

It was 28 August when we were given £5, a pair of boots, a glengarry and two biscuits on which to sleep; no other dress or equipment could be produced. The £5 was spent by about 1,200 of us that same evening and I was billeted out to sleep in a pigsty for the first three weeks. I must say I did not need an alarm clock on those early days, and being a biscuit short, sleep did not come easily.

The camp at Bowlee was now ready and we all reported for duty and now, with the rest of our uniforms, supplied with buttons polished and boots shining, we were called on parade and inspected by the group captain who had previously been the manager of a department store. After inspection, the order came for all airmen holding a current driving licence to take one step forward. My little Austin 7 was safely tucked away, so it was a bit of a shock when I was told to take the train to Cardington and drive back a three ton Crossley and trailer, calling at the ICI plant at Runcorn to pick up hydrogen for the balloon barrage. I did this run for many weeks.

On 4 November 1940, during the blackout, I had a narrow escape when I fell fourteen feet, and woke up two days later in Daveyluilme Military Hospital with a fractured skull. I was a patient for seven weeks, and given twenty eight days' leave, followed by twenty eight days' light duty before going in front of a medical board. They asked me if I could get my job back if I were discharged; the steel company I had worked for had paid me a retainer for the duration. But by this time I loved the service life, so said that I couldn't.

I was now a corporal and proud of the 'A' on my RAF epaulette. Little did I know that I was to lose it when I became commissioned, but it was replaced by a 'VR'. A rather strange thing happened on 30 June 1941: I woke up a corporal, I was a sergeant by midday and a pilot officer by the late afternoon, having paid extra messing in the sergeants' mess at lunch time!

Before going to Tilstock I was posted to Scotland where the station padre took me for a ride at shove-halfpenny; he insisted on playing for 2s. 6d. a time and beat me every time. I found out later that he was the local champion. My posting to Tilstock was to be the best I could have wished for, with Group Captain Harman in charge, and I made lifelong friends with the PFO Flight Lieutenant Jack Bramhall. Nor must I forget Fire Officer Tawnhill who, after one of his frequent cycle trips to Whitchurch, managed to wander off the road and into a bush, which somehow dislodged his false teeth, and a search party had to be organised so that he could eat lunch the next day!

Jack Bramhall and I became great friends; I used to do the time-keeping for him at Ternhill when he had a team of boxers there, and we used to go shooting at the bombing range.

In those days quite a lot of time was spent at the Raven, a public house across the road from the camp, and also at Witchbowl, a café which had a swimming pool. We delighted in those places but I visited them some time ago and couldn't get out quick enough. My days at Tilstock will live for ever; I was surrounded by efficient RAF and WAAF NCOs who, I am sure, kept any slight mistakes made by the personnel in my section well hidden from the officer in command — me. I know this is true as I learnt about it recently at the annual reunion of the MT drivers at Whitchurch. I heard about a certain MT WAAF driver who drove her lorry into a ditch because she did not like the run to Sleap, our satellite airfield. However, I salute the drivers who had to take aircrew and equipment out to dispersal areas at night amongst taxi-ing aircraft with practically no vehicle lights in bad visual conditions.

When 1665 HCU came to Tilstock I was given my second ring to flight lieutenant and very proud too of the promotion, but the days at the unit were numbered and I was posted to Base HQ, Bombay.

8

'DINGLE' O'NEILL

In 1939 I was happily settled with an army family as a nanny to their four children. We had planned that I should go out to India with them, but before the date arrived war was declared, so these plans were cancelled and I took a post with another army family who were then living in Kent.

While I was there I witnessed daily dog fights over the fields of Kent during the summer and autumn of 1940 and the reality of war came home to me. My elder brother was killed on a thousand bomber raid over Germany in March 1942.

It was this that started the train of events that brings me to be writing this story about my time in the WAAF. I was heartbroken and I suppose I felt that in some small way I could hit back.

I faced a selection board in Hastings. While I was there I had walked around the town and down towards the beach to look at the barbed wire entanglement but high brick walls had been built across the ends of the streets leading to the front. Of course we had all heard of these anti-invasion schemes but it was a queer feeling to see it.

I went in to see the committee, armed with what I thought was quite an impressive array of Red Cross certificates, hoping to be chosen as medical orderly, but it was not to be, for at the end of my interview a lady declared, 'Sorry but we have plenty of medical orderlies, but we do need drivers, so that is what you will be.'

I did try to say that I could not drive and had no idea of what went on under the bonnet of a vehicle, but they all smiled and said, 'That is how we like them, we will train you.'

With that I returned to my place of work in Kent, collected all my belongings, including my precious bicycle, and set off home to Shropshire to put my mother in the picture as to all that had happened. The journey across London with my assortment of luggage I shall gloss over except to mention that several times I was tempted to abandon even the bike. I duly arrived home in Shropshire where I spent several weeks with Mum. She was so happy to have my company as my younger brother had by now joined the army.

When my papers arrived with instructions to report to Innsworth, I have to admit to mixed feelings. Regrets at leaving my mother, who had been a widow for many years; also apprehensions about the unknown future. But there was a sense of adventure also.

We must have looked a motley crowd as we arrived at our appointed place. Such confusion and so many instructions. But after a meal we were allocated a bed and everyone was glad to assemble the three squares known as biscuits which, with an assortment of grey blankets, turned into a cocoon of sorts to snuggle into. I could hear the odd sniffle after lights out, as we were all feeling a little homesickness stealing over us. Eventually all was quiet and after fitfully sleeping for what seemed like an eternity, all hell broke loose. It turned out to be a tannoy calling us to be dressed. We were all to get used to this rude awakening in later weeks but on that first morning we must have looked comical as we reacted in different ways. As I sat in my bed, viewing my surroundings, a girl came out of a small corner room and introduced herself as sergeant of the hut. I listened to her friendly speech of welcome and the instructions about what we were to do but I could not help but think about her strange choice of nightwear. She was wearing what I thought were men's blue and white striped pyjamas. But I didn't think that way for long. By the next bedtime we were all attired in the same garments, which proved to be very warm and comfortable.

The next few days were very hectic. We queued continuously

68

Peggy Drummond-Hay on her first leave in 1943.

Jack Heuff, a Canadian soldier stationed at Selsey Bill, 1942-3.

This mark III Stirling (1665 HCU) at Tilstock, overshot the runway and landed on the Whitchurch to Shrewsbury Road, in June 1944. The Stirling was first allocated to 196 Squadron.
(Ray Glass)

Marjorie Cliff, Tilstock.

Marjorie standing on one of the mobile flashing beacons, Tilstock.

Dingle O'Neill.

Frank O'Neill, who was a despatch rider at Tilstock.

Tilstock: Nicky 1st left, Peggy 3rd left, Beryl 4th left
Joan & Cpl. Henry back row.

At Tilstock: All that remains of the Motor Transport rest room in 1986.
2 bays in background.

Vernon on right with his navigator by the tail of their Lancaster when
he went to 7 Squadron P.F.F.

Ron Minchin, who was in the Royal Australian Air Force, in 1943. He joined 196 squadron after his HCU at Woolfox Lodge.

Rosemary's husband, Mac looking at his radio set in his Stirling.

Tilstock: One of our first reunions in 1969
Left to right — Dilys, Betty, Marjorie, Rosemary, Grace,
Pat, Chris and Jackie.

Peter was posted to an island in the Red Sea called Kamaran
for a short time — 'Land of two moons'.

for issue of uniform and kit, medical inspections and jobs. Next came a variety of lectures on every subject, from life in the WAAF to VD.

When all these procedures had been completed, we packed our kit bags, collected a packed meal and boarded a troop train, destination Morecambe, for our square-bashing training. We travelled through the night and arrived in pouring rain, to be marshalled on the front to receive our billet's address. I think that there were twelve girls in our billet and the landlady drew our attention to her list of rules. It was a mighty list, which covered everything. We were comfortable enough there but it was Spartan, to put it kindly.

Each day we assembled on the front to be trained in the art of marching. We were a pathetic looking squad and our instructor wore a permanently pained expression but her daily assured us that we would eventually 'do it her way'. We spent Christmas here, after a series of jabs to complete our misery at being away from home. At last the day came when we passed out on our drill and got postings, where we were to wait for trade training courses. After all the goodbyes I set off for RAF Oakington, near Cambridge. It was a bomber station and I well remember my feeling of awe as I looked up at the huge Stirling bombers. I soon got organised on the formalities and found that I was to live in an old vicarage some distance from camp and transport was organised for us. I enjoyed my stay at Oakington. I had no duties as such; in fact I was a bit of a 'spare file' really, but the MT girls took me about with them on runs to show me the ropes.

This was an operational station and we would gather to watch the bombers returning from raids over Germany. One morning the whole camp turned out to see one parked on a dispersal pan. It was a sight I shall never forget. The fusilage was hanging in great ragged holes and we all marvelled how the pilot had hedgehopped home. I had my twenty-first birthday at Oakington and as it occurred on domestic night, when I was cleaning floors, I really felt a tiny bit cheesed off, but the unbelievable happened. My brother, who was stationed near Northampton, somehow got through on the telephone to the MT Section with birthday wishes to be relayed to me, with plans for us to meet in Cambridge the next day to celebrate; it was a lovely birthday after all. We duly met and had a super day together.

My posting to Blackpool for my trade training at last arrived and I was on my way again. This time my billet in Hornby Road was almost a home from home. There were about sixteen of us in this house and it must have seemed like an invasion but we were made very welcome with many late night cuppas enjoyed in the kitchen with the family.

Our training was to be at the Ribble Garage and at the appointed hour we formed up in squads in Hornby Road and marched off to start our new way of life. The mornings were spent in the classrooms learning about engines and in the afternoons we learned to drive. Fordson lorries were something of a challenge and the roads around that area reverberated to the noise of novices trying to change gear. We also learned convoy driving round the roads out towards Garstang. What joy it was to move onto staff cars! Eventually order came out of chaos and most of us passed our driving tests. There was considerable excitement when our postings were announced. I was to go to 81 OTU at Prees Heath, which was known as RAF Tilstock. Once more it was all farewells. We had made good friends here and we hated saying goodbye.

I went home on leave, very proud of my uniform and of my achievements so far. Prees Heath was in Shropshire so I was able to hitchhike home fairly regularly, once I was settled in and organised. We lived in huts, about twenty to each one, and everyone cycled everywhere on the camp. It was a friendly section at the MT yard and I soon felt at home. Another WAAF from Blackpool was also posted here and we became good friends and still are to this day. It rained for weeks and everywhere was a sea of mud. Our rest room in the early days was a caravan but later we got a permanent hut. On reporting for duty on the first morning, I was somewhat taken aback to read by my name on the blackboard 'Funeral Duty'. I inquired what this meant and was told to report to the morgue at the sick bay with a lorry to collect two coffins, then to return to the guard room to form up in procession with a coach, containing firing party,

70

bearers, camera party and staff car with an officer party and then to proceed to Chester Cemetery for the funerals. This seemed a bit much on my first day but sadly I did it several times while serving at Tilstock. These were men from the Commonwealth countries who were killed in flying accidents while training on our drome. I recently visited the cemetery; it was a strange feeling to think that I had driven some of those lads to their last resting place.

Most of our days were spent doing routine jobs. Driving the coaches around the airfield delivering crews to their aircraft on the dispersal pans and collecting other crews as they landed was one such job. Delivering coke with the help of POWs, collecting ashes or delivering water in a tanker were others and everyone's favourite job was driving a flat trailer collecting lavatory buckets and taking them to the sewage farm! I used to lock myself in the cab and light a cigarette as the POWs rode on the steps.

Our job was so varied we never got bored. We took coachloads of aircrew to Fenns Moss where they practised dinghy drill, which was most entertaining. Some days we drove out to the field where the aircraft practised container dropping. These containers all had to be retrieved if you were on flarepath duty at night, (and I have known the wind to change half a dozen times). You spent all night with the crew, collecting up the lamps from the runway in use and laying a new flarepath and then having to repeat the performance at each wind change. One job I did not like was driving what was known as the trafficator van. You drove in front of a taxi-ing aircraft, flashing instructions to the pilot with lights. One of our girls had a very close brush with death when the aircraft that she was guiding overran her van and the back was crushed.

A great deal of time was spent driving back and forth to our satellite camp at Sleap. I particularly remember one journey at night. I had a panic message to take a wing commander to Sleap, as an aircraft was in trouble. We did the trip in record time and I was fascinated by the cool way he took charge. He told the pilot to cruise round to use up his fuel and then issued detailed instructions as to what to do, ending up with, 'Now you sever the oil pipe and the undercarriage will come down and lock.' Which it duly did and they landed safely. I was thrilled to be there and everyone cheered when the lads walked out. The boy who had cut the pipe was covered in oil. The wing commander turned to me and said, 'Come on driver, you deserve a flying breakfast too.' Bacon and eggs never tasted so good.

We all enjoyed a long run — journeys away from base — with no signposts anywhere and masks on the headlights, reducing the beam to mere slits. I sometimes wonder how we ever arrived at the right place. I once went to Newark with a lorryload of 'nickel', (propaganda pamphlets to the laymen). Before leaving the camp I had to collect an armed guard to accompany me. We had strict instructions: no hitchhikers and we must never take our eyes off the lorry at the same time, whether it be for a cuppa or to answer the call of nature.

Rumours were rife about the forthcoming D-Day and one morning I was told to prepare the big staff car, to collect my overnight bag and to report to the officers' mess to pick up a party of four who I was to take to a hush-hush destination on Salisbury Plain. It was all so secret, the sergeant could hardly bring himself to tell me where I was supposed to go! To this day I cannot remember the name of the camp but I collected my senior officers and we were off. Lovely, I thought, a coveted long run, and I knew we would stop for a nice meal en route, all paid for by my passengers. We duly arrived at our venue and off I went to report to find a bed. Such a crowd of drivers from all over the country I had never seen before. The speculating that went on was really something as we began to realise the size of the party of top brass that we had assembled in this place. Then we were told later that the camp had been sealed and this was it at last. I hardly slept. I kept wondering if my brother was sitting in one of the tanks I had noticed in groups under every patch of trees on the way over the Plain. There is no need for me to relate the events of 6 June but whenever I cross Salisbury Plain now, I relive that day. We later returned to our camps to one topic of conversation only, the D-Day landings.

It was during my time at Tilstock that I met my husband.

He was our despatch rider and we hit if off right away. He had been in aircrew but was grounded after a long battle against nausea when flying so he came to Tilstock as our DR. It was fate and later we decided to get married.

Our send-off was something we shall always remember. We held it in a village pub. All our section came and crowds we did not even know. The landlady produced sandwiches and goodies and a squadron leader whom we knew played the piano all evening. I can still see his pints of beer stretching from one end of the piano to the other. They were a wonderful crowd; they had organised a whip-round and bought us two blankets and a carving set which, in those days, was somewhat of an achievement. We still have those treasured presents in use forty-nine years on.

We were married on 24 July, 1944 in the village church at my home. Despite all wartime rationing and shortages, my mother, helped by various aunts, cousins and friends, produced a reception and party in the village hall that left us speechless. Literally everyone in our village came to join in and the only regret that we had was that my brother could not be with us to give me away; he was now in France. We spent our honeymoon in Oxford as guests of my aunt and cousins who had planned trips and a theatre visit, etc. It was a precious week that flew by and we almost forgot that we were at war, but all too soon we had to return to our unit.

Things changed. Now we were allowed to live off camp in the village of Prees and we could not have been more fortunate in our choice of digs. Our landlady, a spinster, was a dear, and insisted on mothering us. We were very spoiled. We cycled into work at the camp each day. It was a familiar sight to see airforce personnel on bikes in those country lanes. Life settled into a pattern. Our duties did not always coincide but on the whole it worked out well. I took my driving test for coaches round the narrow back streets of Whitchurch; I passed and so became a leading aircraftswoman. It was with great pride that I sewed on my propellor flashes.

There was a real stir in the camp when Anne Shelton came to entertain us. The cinema was packed that night. Sometimes we would have a whip round the MT Section and have a shindig at the Raven Hotel on the edge of the airfield. Those were great evenings with everyone doing their favourite party pieces. Now this may seem frivolous to our readers but it helped to ease our sad times: for instance, when we drove a coach full of laughing, singing lads to a base down south to replenish lost crews, only to find out three days later, when we returned with another load, that some of those boys were already missing; we felt their loss deeply.

When I arrived at 81 OTU they had Whitleys and Wellingtons but later, when 1665 HCU came, there were Stirlings and Halifaxes to train crews for towing gliders for airborne troops. It was exciting to watch all this but sadly we had accidents with resulting casualties. It was not my favourite job to drive the ambulance on these occasions. I suppose our worst time was in September 1943 when a Whitley crashed into the control at Sleap, killing several, including two of our WAAF drivers. We were shattered.

On a lighter note, a sight that I found quite awe-inspiring was to watch one of our corporals setting off around those narrow lanes with his circus, as we called it, which was a huge Thorneycroft lorry, towing a flashing beacon trailer, towing his accommodation caravan. To my knowledge the only time he had any sort of mishap was when a vehicle scraped him whilst parked outside Wem post office.

In February I had a severe ear infection from swimming and spent weeks in the Ear, Nose and Throat Hospital at Shrewsbury. While I was there my brother was wounded at the Rhine crossing and had been flown home to a hospital in Bradford. I managed to get discharged and whilst on sick leave my husband and I set off to find him. He was in St. Luke's Hospital and in bad shape. We spent our leave with him and on return to base I looked up one of our drivers, whose home was in Bradford, to ask if she could help in any way. Her family were incredible. They visited the hospital, took goodies and best of all they invited my mother and my brother's widow to go and stay with them as long as they wished. Such wonderful things only happened in wartime.

After victory in Europe, married women were the first to be offered discharge, so when my turn came it was with sadness that I said goodbye to my wonderful friends. I could write reams about my life in the WAAF and the day to day funny things that happened, but one chapter is my allotted portion. So I shall finish by saying the very best thing that has come out of all this is my marriage — we are now heading for a golden wedding — and the fact that we have a reunion each May back near the Prees camp where we are still able to go into our hut and ablutions known by us as our pilgrimage.

We shall be lifelong friends, a very special relationship which even our children cannot quite comprehend. When we arrive at the hotel the other guests stare as each ex-WAAF throws her arms round my elderly husband and kisses him; he wouldn't miss our get-together for anything. We relive those days all over again with everyone saying, 'Do you remember. . .?'

9

FRANK O'NEILL

I became a member of the RAF in 1941. It would have been earlier had I not been in reserved occupation, working at the ironstone mines at Scunthorpe in Lincolnshire. I volunteered for aircrew and was attested at Birmingham.

Some weeks later I was called to arms, spending some time at RAF Catfoss in Yorkshire as a jack of all trades awaiting a course for air gunners. I was posted with sixteen others to a new drome in Yorkshire as general duty wallahs to get the drome ready for the real occupation. This was a good number until the day the two officers, a flight lieutenant and a pilot officer, decided that my mate and I should be mess waiters.

Life was pretty miserable as they had three meals a day with dinner at eight o'clock in the evening, after which there was the washing up to do, the mess to be cleaned and polished etc. So I decided that it was time for a change. When I served the soup I carried the plate with my thumb very conspicuously in it. When I put the plate down in front of the pilot officer I sucked my thumb loudly. Meanwhile Denny, my mate, managed to get a large amount of coffee in the saucers. I think that they must have been planning to get rid of us, for the next day we were told 'from now on you horrible pair will be on picket duty'. This was a good number, twenty-four hours on, twenty-four hours off, but this only lasted a week. Then came my posting to ITW at Bridlington for aircrew square-bashing and examinations. I really enjoyed the square-bashing as aircrew cadets marched at 140 paces per minute, the same as army light infantry and we all were as keen as mustard to impress the local female population. It was a sight to see when even after a long march the PTI would say, 'bags of swank now,' as we reached the end of the road.

Eventually I and the rest of my squad were posted to Dalcross in Scotland to No. 3 Air Gunnery School. Here we were treated as special, to be trained by air-gunners who had done at least one tour or more. They knew what it was all about and were going to pass on all their knowledge to us. We flew in Boulton Paul Defiants. I passed in all my exams, except the flying. Something lacking caused me to be violently sick each time I was airborne. I thought that it might have got better when I got onto bigger planes so I cadged rides with some Yanks flying Oxfords. This was mostly doing circuits and bumps. But it was to no avail. I went before the medical officer and he had reports from my pilots and instructors and I was told that I would cease training and be posted to Blackpool to await my discharge.

This unit at Blackpool were all ex-aircrew trainees. Some had been in crashes, others had misbehaved in some fashion such as low flying and aerobatics. As we were all volunteers we were told that we would be discharged. This did not happen, of course, as you were asked if you would like to try another trade. Those who said yes were given a list to choose from with no guarantee that your choice would be respected. I suspect that the ones who said no were held back until the other services could accommodate them.

I spent several weeks drilling and marching about Blackpool, all of us very low in spirits at having missed out on our fondest dreams. Eventually I was one of the lucky ones and got the posting that I had chosen to go to RAF Weedon to train as a despatch rider. I had now been in the service for about ten months and knew my way around. I had never owned a motorcycle but I could ride one reasonably well because my best friend had one and had no compunction in lending me his Panther. But, as I was saying, I knew my way around and there is nothing an instructor likes better than to take a complete novice and turn him into his star pupil. Pity the one who knows it all, hears all, 'know nowt' is a good way of getting the instructor on your side. I eventually passed out AC 2 despatch rider and was posted to RAF Finningly in Yorkshire. That was quite a long introduction, perhaps too long, but I need to explain why I am writing in service women's memoirs by giving some background about who I am and what I was doing.

I only had a month or so at Finningly when I was attached, (that's a charming word), to Burcotes, the satellite. Six months later I was posted to RAF Whitchurch, later called RAF Tilstock. I arrived at Tilstock, as I shall call it from now on. It was raining and did so for what seems like weeks. Tilstock was known as 81 OTU and was a large camp with lots of bods, about 1-2,000 eventually, but the MT Section was understaffed. People were still coming and going; this maniacal desire to stop people from getting roots seems to spring from somebody having a pin and sticking it in a list of names and it is moving time for some poor soul.

The WAAF drivers, if you could recognise them as female in that monsoon weather, had a caravan as a rest room, which was a good thing in a way as it was just above water level. The reason it was difficult to pick out the sex of the person who floated by us was because of the good old groundsheet, completely waterproof and making a shape that successfully directed all the rain off your shoulders and into your boots. Some of the WAAF drivers had come from Finningly, but no one that I knew. I first began to appreciate and get to know well the ones who said, 'Would you like some tea?' This was in pint mugs as black as a railway tunnel, (the tea, not the mugs), several spoons of sugar obtained by much nefarious scheming and topped by large doses of tinned milk known to put hair on one's chest. Coming back off a despatch run, cold and very wet, it made things better. Even the most hardened WAAF seemed to give a soft, soothing smile when I returned in those conditions. The other despatch rider did not need comforting; he was older and well in with the NCO, IC transport who looked after its own. (There's a thought, was I the WAAF's own?)

One day the old despatch driver was posted and his place was taken by Orville Phillips, a great lad the same age as myself.

78

He and I became great mates and when one was on duty the other was standby. So we took the Met report run alternately. These runs at least four times a day were about sixteen to twenty miles to our satellite in RAF Sleap.

A great change had taken place in my life. I was walking out with one of the WAAF drivers. We met at work and whenever we were off duty together, and what started as just a date turned into love. After quite a long courtship we decided to get married, despite all the wartime difficulties we had, and thanks to my very dear mother-in-law, it was a most wonderful wedding. Getting all the guests together and bedded down was a major operation as they came from all different parts of the country and trains and buses were difficult to come by. I cycled into Bridgnorth from my wife's home, eight miles of up hill and down dale, riding one bike and pushing another, for one of our WAAF friends who I met at Bridgnorth. Then I turned and set off eight miles back. (Oh halcyon days of super fitness!)

Back at camp after a short honeymoon and back to the nitty gritty, it all was the same, except for myself. I was and still am extremely happy with my partner.

I was duty DR one day, a miserable cold day and had had one run after another — only short but important distances. Each time that I arrived back at base and was relaxing with a cuppa, I was called out again. After about the fifth time Orville, who was on standby, said he would do the run. Away he went and had only just left when another run came for the same place. I decided to try and catch my mate up, so went with great speed down the country lanes. Just before I got to Wem I saw a very smashed motor cycle. I went some distance past and then realised that it had been Orville's bike. I went back as fast as I could, the accident had happened outside an American army camp. I was taken into the camp hospital. Orville was on the operating table in a dreadful state and died quite soon. To say I was shattered is a very great understatement. There was an American soldier outside waiting for me; he was only about nineteen and suffering from shock. He was able to tell me that Orville came round the bend in the middle of the road and he was also in the middle and they had met head on. I think no blame can be placed on anyone, it was a combination of circumstances: Orville doing me a favour, an unskilled GI and fate.

My wife was on airfield duty coach driving when someone had said that the duty despatch rider had just been killed. Knowing that I was duty DR she presumed it was me and immediately dashed to the MT Section and naturally was delighted that I was still alive but saddened that Orville was gone. But life goes on, sometimes smoothly other times rocky.

I had fourteen days' jankers for burning down the rest room by accident, I hasten to add. It happened when I put a petrol-soaked rag on a fire I thought was out, but a belch of fire came out of the bottom on the stove and it spread very quickly. The crash tender arrived, also the station commander in his car. I was standing watching the fire crew when the group captain said to me, 'Who is responsible for this?' to which I replied 'I am, sir,' standing smartly to attention. He told me to shut up and asked the SWO to arrest and charge me. I was taken away not unkindly, for the SWO was one I had done a bit of shopping for on some of my trips.

I came up before the squadron leader, admin who remanded me to the group captain, as it was too serious an offence to be dealt with by a squadron leader. By this time it was beginning to sound as if I would be sent to the glasshouse. I was marched into the group captain's office. He gave me a severe dressing down and finished by saying, 'I am not going to punish you for what you did, but,' he paused and gave a little smile, and then I spoiled it all and smiled back. He continued, 'but for what you might have done, fourteen days CB.' I think I was very lucky; fourteen days' jankers was easy enough in comparison to the glasshouse.

My wife was responsible for getting me to drive, when I was waiting for her to finish duty. The last thing to be done was the dispersing of some of the lorries in case of air raids. This could take quite a time and she showed me how to work the clutch, gears and especially the brakes and then we would disperse together.

I was sometimes given camp driving jobs after taking a test and one of these was sanitation waggon duties. Italian

POWs emptied the latrine buckets into a trough at the back of the lorry, then they banged on the side to tell the driver to set a suction pump to blow and that spread it about thirty yards over the sewage beds. One very hot day I was on duty outside HQ. I was in the cab reading a newspaper when a POW banged for the pump. I kicked it with my foot and revved the engine. I heard much shouting and one of the POWs came to the door, covered with lavatory paper etc. I switched off and was a bit upset at the scene outside. The POWs were somewhat upset also, especially as they had the cleaning up to do. I could not help thinking of that favourite service song, *Sweet Violets*.

When there were a lot of parcels for the DR's run a girl driver took me in a van. On one occasion driving back to camp in the dark, a lorry with a bulldozer on the back met us and sliced the top of the van off. Fortunately no one was hurt. I received a cut hand picking part of the van roof off the road. The driver was a bit shocked but not too bad. The lorry driver was in a bit of a state because his load was overhanging and should not have been on the road at night.

On a wet and misty November evening I had to report to the padre. He wanted a bottle of sacramental wine delivered to Hawkstone Priory. I stuffed the bottle in my flat leather despatch case but the top would not close because of the height and off I went, not over joyed at having to go after a wet miserable day. I went at great speed and made a mess of getting round an S-bend. The footrest caught the road and I slid sideways. Then a miracle happened. I lay there and watched the wine fly through the air and land on top of the hedge. I gathered up wine and bike and did the delivery. On arrival I rang a bell at a massive door. A monk answered and insisted that I go in. He made me sit at a table and fetched a mug of tea and a massive piece of fruit cake, then left me to my refreshments and to drip water all over the polished floor. I waited some time but he never came back, so I let myself out. What struck me at the time was how clean he was. Perhaps it was because I was so wet and dirty.

I could go on and on but I am sure you will have had enough

'VI-N' Airborne — Target Hawkstone Priory

of my memories by now. I will finish by saying what a remarkable experience it was, being with such a mixture of people. Sadness and great joy came in spasms, but most of all a comradeship that is never repeated anywhere else.

I am very lucky. I gained a wife and host of friends, male and female, and I still go to WAAF reunions and find new memories to talk over each time we meet. Our hair is grey or white, but when we meet the eyes are sparkling just like the old days and we reminisce and swear that we see the same young faces all round us.

10

SPUD MURPHY (DORIS NOW WALKER)

1942

I have early memories of square-bashing on Morecambe Pier, in midwinter, chin straps down and ground sheets hugged tightly round, hating the WAAF drill sergeant like mad!

They used to call it 'square-bashing'. The only thing they wanted to bash was the DRILL SERGEANT!

There was a three months', driving course at Ribble Garage in Blackpool. Those were the days, in billets with a Mrs Monks, mean old ladies who half starved us young, hungry brats. The rooms were full of aspidistras, which we tried in vain to kill off with tea or anything to hand!

I had a hilarious driving course, my ginger instructor dressed entirely in ginger and with ginger hair; he needed it for pluck! I do hope he is still alive, he was a real comedian. I couldn't keep my foot off the clutch so he tied some string round my foot and gave it a jerk every so often! He used to encourage us to pass the army lorries, also learners. He would say, 'Put your foot down and pass this lot,' then pull his ginger hat down over his eyes!

But we didn't kill it Mrs Monks, your tea did!

The Tower Ballroom and the Winter Gardens were the highlight of the course, and we spent most evenings enjoying ourselves! The Blackpool folk must have crossed the roads at their peril in those dark days!

On to RAF Marham, King's Lynn — I used to see the Mosquitoes taking off for Germany. Eventually I was posted to Waterbeach 1665 HCU. I arrived to find a bunch of raw driving recruits the same as me, eighteen and with very little experience of driving; we all did our best! Fancy free and away from our mums, looking for excitement. I fear it was always the passengers who got the excitement! With us girls crashing about in our lorries — those thirty hundredweight Fords — the gear change could be heard for miles!

Many stories could be told: the WAAF who made everyone get out and help turn the van round — she couldn't find reverse! Another WAAF who let a persistent fellow 'have a go at driving'. He drove right through a hut, with airmen still in bed!

At Woolfox Lodge, I used to swim in the lake. The airmen made a big raft on floating drums which we used to dive off. On reaching land, we would find the men had tied wire round the bottom of our trousers and the cuffs, so we couldn't get into them!

A real mucky airfield, Woolfox. The MT yard was the old farmyard; the lorries and drivers were constantly covered in mud! I remember Peggy and I walking past SP Grant and stamping in the puddles as we got to the guardroom — so we covered him in mud as well — we were always threatened with a 'fizzer'. I drove the dustcart one day with two Irishmen who kept telling me to back-up and up and up. This was on top of a large pit. Back I went and down and disappeared into the bowels of the earth. The MT had to come out with a crane to get the lorry out. Again I was threatened with a 'fizzer'.

Once I was told to go and collect the flashing beacon, which was kept behind the guard room. I hooked it up and towed it away, taking the fence round the guard room with me. In the mirror I could see the SPs waving their arms, but I just put my foot down.

We moved to Tilstock in a year, and then on to beautiful Yorkshire. How I loved driving around the countryside — I

Time for reflection! SP takes offence as DMT takes a fence.

still have a great love for the country! Yorkshire with its cobbled industrial towns and its great open spaces. York, with the chocolate workers leaning on the vans at the traffic lights, and the great market at Leeds!

One winter's night some German prisoners escaped, so the airmen had to occupy the aircraft, in case a German pinched it! I had to take food and tea out in the lorry. It was the early hours in the morning, thick snow. I was walking back to the lorry and suddenly it was so quiet and still, no noise, no sound, nothing, I became terrified! I jumped into the lorry and drove off, never being so scared.

The war continued with plenty of night flying practice — Stirlings and gliders and tow hooks whizzing down, not forgetting the container-dropping — usually in a nearby lake. Never a dull moment for the WAAF driver!

Well, after four years as a WAAF, I came out with a husband and also a very glowing report of service — a bit of a tall one I feel, but it does seem all so long ago! My grandaughter was onced asked by the teacher at school to take some photos of old people — I gave her one of myself in WAAF uniform! But it's funny, I don't feel that old!

11

JACKY HARLEY (NOW BURNE)

In the first year of war I worked as a shorthand typist in the goods yard department of the railway unit until I was conscripted into the WAAF.

I had to report to RAF Innsworth in Gloucestershire and my mother, who was heartbroken at losing her 'baby', came as far as Wolverhampton with me, as it was the first time I had been away from home on my own and I was rather apprehensive. I don't remember much of the journey or arriving at the camp, except for having to line up with the other girls and being marched off to our respective huts and my feet were like ice, it being so cold. I couldn't get to sleep and just wanted to go home to Mum! The next morning, having to get up early to the icy ablutions and go over to the mess for soggy bacon and baked beans, was a rotten start to my WAAF services. During the day we had to march to the equipment section to be issued with our kit, then back to the hut to put it on and have a laugh at each other because nothing fitted. Afterwards we had to parcel up our civilian clothes and march down to the post office to send them home. My mother wrote to me, telling me that she saw the postman coming down the road on his bicycle with the sleeve of my dress hanging out! Every morning we had baked beans and got used to them or go hungry!

I was then posted to Morecambe with a few other WAAFs. Here we did our basic training, marching up and down the seafront going to lectures and having medical inspections such as FFIs. We were billeted in a nice house and had quite good food; I had a pleasant room at the top of the house but it was very cold. When I first saw the WAAF-issue flannel pyjamas I said in no way was I going to wear those, but they were very warm and I overcame my pride in the end! I had a big double bed which I had to strip down every morning. This seemed a complete waste of time and the girl in the next room never did hers — how she got away with it I don't know! Her name was Sylvia. We became quite good friends and we were posted to South Wales with six other girls when we finished our square-bashing. It was a remote place in the middle of nowhere called Talbenny, about fourteen miles from Milford Haven and the same distance from Haverfordwest. It was a flying boat base with a Polish squadron (304 Squadron). It was a very new camp; some of the buildings were uncompleted and it was very dispersed. We slept the first night in a hut with no doors at either end and no furniture or fittings, so we pushed our beds together and pulled our bedding over our heads because we could hear mice running about! It came as no real surprise that we had to wash under a pump in the field which adjoined a clifftop overlooking the sea. Not a good place in the middle of November, but I think we were beginning to get toughened up!

After that Sylvia and I were moved into the WAAF Queen Bee's quarters to be batwomen. This turned out to be quite a cushy job and she was really very sweet. There didn't seem to be much discipline there and we had some smashing dances and I really fancied the drummer in the band. We went out quite often and whenever I hear *Moonlight and Roses* — the band's signature tune — I still think fondly of him.

I spent my twenty-first birthday in the guardroom on duty. It was pouring with rain and the roof was leaking. I don't know why they bothered with a guardroom as we used to book in and then go out again through a hole in the hedge! By this time I was getting used to being away from home. I thoroughly enjoyed Christmas at Talbenny and decided that I would enjoy being in the services. Before going to Blackpool on the driving course I was given seven days' leave to go home. At Blackpool I was billeted in 98 Hornby Road and shared a room with Jill. We used to go out together in the evenings, mostly to the Tower Ballroom where the WAAF outnumbered the chaps by about fifty to one we didn't get asked for a dance very much. Not that there was much room to dance!

When the time came for me to get behind the steering wheel for the first time I was very nervous but after a few times round Stanley Park I was thrilled to bits and wrote home saying that I could drive. I liked driving much better than the theory which, to be honest, I don't think I fully understood and it was a good job we didn't have to rely on it too much later on. We used to go out in the country in convoy, two drivers to a car, and one day when my co-driver was at the wheel, she swerved and ended up hitting a tree. The instructor was not very pleased and kept on sucking his bismuth tablets for indigestion, which was frequent with our erractic driving, but he was a very helpful chap on the whole!

Sometimes we had to drive out to a very steep but short hill, where we had to practice changing down at the bottom to take a sharp corner and also do handbrake starts. It was known to us as Heartbreak Hill. As well as driving, we had to do loads of marching and the weather was then bitterly cold. The sergeant in charge of us was called Sergeant Hurry-Up because he was always saying 'Come on, you horrible lot — hurry up — swing them arms, up-two-three-up-two-three.'

It was Easter Monday when I took my test on lorries. I think the whole world was in Blackpool that day, but I managed to pass and didn't knock anyone down in the process! At the end of the course, we were all posted to different stations. I was posted to RAF Tilstock along with LACW Hinton, later to be known as Dingle because she frequently called everything 'Dingleberry'.

We became good friends and were billeted in the same hut where our beds were next to each other. We spent quite a few twenty-four hour passes at my home and my mother used to make us cakes and give us soap to take back to camp, which was a luxury as it was rationed in those days. Once we decided to go to the cinema at Shrewsbury on our way back to camp at Tilstock. After about half an hour in the cinema the man

90

sitting next to me started groping my leg so I got up in a bad temper and rushed out, leaving poor Dingle running after me, wondering what had happened. We had a good laugh about it later on.

After three weeks at Tilstock a new MT officer arrived to take over the section, Flying Officer Burne. My first driving job was to go to SHQ and bring back a staff car for servicing to the MT yard. At SHQ a Squadron Leader Scott asked me to take him to his section near MT but I couldn't get the car started and got in a bit of a panic. I eventually managed to get it going and dropped my passenger off at his section. Much to my consternation, I was reported by him to the MT officer for my inefficiency in not being able to start the car, but nothing further was said about it — not a very good start to my driving duties. My first run off the station was a bit of a disaster because I arrived at Stafford railway thinking I was detailed to pick up two officers from the train, but when I arrived two RAF types met me and started to look under the seats asking, 'Where are they?' It transpired that I should have taken two officers from Tilstock to the station, and so I had to do the run all over again. It took quite a long time to live it down, but at least they did see the funny side of it. I also remember being torn off a strip for driving on the grass to avoid an aircraft. So what? Didn't we all have to survive.

I did my first night duty with Dingle. We used to sleep in a caravan and I remember how frightened we were when the duty airmen said we had to go through an initiation ceremony, which meant we had to be de-bagged. However they were only joking, and the duty was uneventful. One night on duty Dingle had been to the mess for our rations and had managed to scrounge some bacon and eggs. We decided to do some illegal cooking in the WAAF restroom. We had just got the meal cooking nicely when one of the fitters rushed in to tell us that the messing officer and the MT officer were coming towards the hut. We tried to hide everything but, of course, the smell prevailed. Neither of them said a word but I saw one of them give a sly wink as they were leaving. We used to cook chips in an old tin which had probably contained engine oil, but they tasted good and we never came to any harm.

Our MT dances at the Raven were good fun; I remember drinking a pint of beer in one go simply because Sergeant Powell said I couldn't do it! I don't remember much about climbing over the perimeter fence to get my bicycle but I did find it eventually and somehow rode it back along the perimeter track. My guardian angel must have been with me that night because I didn't meet any aircraft and ended up in the right hut! I lost quite a few bikes but always managed to get a replacement!

I left Tilstock at the end of 1944 and later married the MT officer and we had five lovely sons. We now have seven grand-daughters and one grandson and lots of happy memories.

12

MARJORIE CLIFF (NOW WATERHOUSE)

When war was declared I was nineteen years old and working in a stockbroker's office. I was a volunteer in the local ambulance service and had to turn out every time the sirens sounded. One day I decided to go to the recruiting office in Bradford and volunteer for the WAAF as a driver. My friend had volunteered for the WRENS. It was quite a long time before I received my papers and was on my way to RAF Innsworth in Gloucestershire. I spent a week there learning how to salute, and how to make a service bed and was, of course, kitted out. Our kit, particularly the undies, were beyond belief, knee-length grey wool knickers. After being in the french silk variety they took some getting used to, but the item I found most horrible was our issue pint mug — I ask you!

At the end of the week, we were split up into different trades and dispatched to Morecambe by train to do our square-bashing. We received vaccinations and other innoculations. Our billet was reasonably clean and pleasant, being in requisitioned civilian terraced houses with the typical seaside landlady, who seemed to get enough rations to feed us quite well. We attended several documentary film shows on the background of the RAF. At the end of six weeks us MT hopefuls were sent to No. 1 Driving School at Blackpool and were given first class training by BSM — half days driving and the rest of the day on lectures which included tests on theory. My first exams were completed satisfactorily and the serious part; learning to drive lorries, began.

I don't think there has been a colder winter than January and February 1942 in Blackpool. We had three WAAFs to a lorry, one driving and two sitting in the open back. As we took it in turns to drive around Lancashire in the freezing cold I soon became quite ill and after reporting sick I was told to go to bed. My room in my billet was in the attic of an exceptionally sleazy boarding house, and it was a great relief to be taken by ambulance to the WAAF hospital, which was exceptionally clean and comfortable, with large windows overlooking the sea. It had been the Carlton Hotel previously and was on the promenade. However, I was wakened up by a nursing sister and told to get out of bed, pick up my neatly folded clothes from the chair and hang them on the hook behind the door! My great coat had to be buttoned up with the buttons facing outwards into the room, my hat as though I was wearing it on the peg above and my irons (knife, fork and spoon) and the dreaded pint mug, had to be set out on the marble mantlepiece as well! I had bronchitis and a temperature of 104 degrees!

The next day I was listening to the gramophone when suddenly there was a pounding of feet along the corridor, shouting and screaming. Apparently a WAAF on the wireless course had gone berserk and had got out of her locked room when a meal was being served to her; the tune on the player at the time was *Ave Maria* and every time I hear it, it reminds me of that poor girl. I took my final driving test on Easter Monday and was sent on leave.

I went home. My boyfriend, who I had been going out with for two years, was also on leave but it was embarkation leave for the Far East which was a bit much as he had already been in France and had got back via Dunkirk. He did in fact spend four years in Burma and India with the 14th Army. On this leave he proposed to me.

I was posted to Finningley in Yorkshire, which had been a peacetime station and had good facilities. One of our duties was to lay out the flarepath at the side of the runway with gooseneck flares, pacing out the exact spacing. There were several other dirty jobs like that but we did it in good heart. We were all confined to camp for seven days pending a thousand bomber raid and it was very exciting, even though our aircraft were 'Wimpeys', only on leaflet dropping! We left Finningley after a year when a Polish squadron took over.

Our WAAF MT sergeant chose six of us to go to RAF Tilstock in Shropshire, which had been previously named Whitchurch being near to that town. What a shock it was to be stationed on a wartime base; apart from the runways and hardstanding, the whole place was a sea of mud! We were issued with bicycles, which made it better to get about, and after the wet winter the grass began to grow around the camp. We were all billeted in huts, which meant living closely to each other and forming, as it turned out, lasting friendships. On days off we would snatch an extra hour in bed and someone would bring us a piece of soggy bread or toast and a mug of almost cold tea from the mess.

There were quite a lot of accidents and we were closely involved in the aftermath, taking personnel out to the crash with special equipment or driving the ambulance to the crash or to the cemetery. The cemetery was on the outskirts of Chester and one had to drive through the city to the funeral with the coffins draped in the Union Jack. I did this duty twice, which was enough. I was instrumental in having a 'Stop' sign placed at the junction in the middle of Wem High Street end. One Christmas morning I took the OD padre to Sleap (our satellite) for a church service and as we returned along Wem High Street a farmer driving a van and trailer full of milk came straight out of a side turning and shunted our van across the road. A policeman soon arrived and took the usual statements. Then the CO came along on his way to Sleap and offered to take the padre back to Tilstock for his next service, with the aside to me, 'It's no use crying over spilt milk'.

We had plenty of long distance runs but one I always remember was being sent to the officers' mess to pick up a Squadron Leader Wall to take him to Netheravon in Wiltshire. I had a Commer fifteen hundred weight which was full of armaments. When he saw this he was absolutely fuming as he had expected a staff car and a male driver. So I was ordered back to the MT yard to change driver. However, there were

95

no male drivers available, so he had no option but to have me drive him to Netheravon. After we had gone about two miles he calmed down and from then on we got on well. Our first stop was Worcester, where he bought me a bag of apples (to ease his conscience?) and then he bought lunch for us at Cirencester at the King's Head. We arrived at Netheravon in time for his meeting and I delivered the weapons to the armoury. On the return journey he insisted that we had dinner in Oxford and when I dropped him off at the officer's mess at Tilstock, he thanked me for a most enjoyable day!

The war finally ended and my boyfriend returned from India and fixed a date for our wedding — 12 February 1946. I was demobbed on 5 January. My parents were just wonderful about us getting married and gave us a first class wedding even at such short notice. Two years later we were blessed with twin daughters!

I will never forget my days in the WAAF and every year I look forward to our reunion at Whitchurch, where we have a special time with special friends and tramp around the old airfield.

13

GRACE WOOLHAM (NOW SUDDABY)

At the outbreak of the Second World War I was living with my
parents and brothers in the village of Prees in North Shropshire,
five miles south of Whitchurch. I worked at home doing all the
jobs one has to do around the house. I also helped with the
outside jobs as we had milking cows, pigs and hens as well as
a butcher's shop, so there was always plenty to do.

When we knew that we were to have an aerodrome on Prees
Heath, our local beauty spot, we had mixed feelings. The airfield
was opened in 1942 and was originally called Whitchurch Heath,
but this later changed to Tilstock. However, I'd better go back
to the beginning.

It was in November 1941 that I joined the WAAF. I went
by train from Whitchurch to Innsworth, where I was issued with
my uniform, took part in a mock gas attack, learnt how to make
my bed and fold my blankets in the air force fashion. We all
stayed there for four days, after which we all moved to
Morecambe, a train full of us. The journey took all day after
being shunted several times into sidings. When we finally arrived
we were taken to our billets. We lived in houses, twelve to a
house. I don't remember the road or the name of the landlady,
but she was very kind to us and the house was comfortable. It
was here that square-bashing began, which in fact I enjoyed.
The corporal was reasonable and my shoes were comfortable
so I didn't mind marching up and down the promenade.

After Morecambe I was moved to Weeton for my driving

97

course. It was a very cold winter there and keeping our hut warm was a continual problem. As well as the stove in the hut, we had a coke brazier in the ablutions which we had to stoke up; it was always going out and lighting it again was awful. We used to go down to the MT yard and push a piece of rag into the petrol tank of any vehicle we could find, then race back to the ablutions, hoping we wouldn't be caught. It usually did the trick but I sometimes wonder how we didn't blow the place up! The course here consisted of driving in the mornings and theory in the afternoons. As far as I can remember we all passed and we were then allowed home for the weekend.

On our return we expected to be posted to stations but no one seemed to want us, so we were sent down to London and billeted in a block of flats. After reporting to Admin each morning we were free for the day. This went on for about two weeks; then one day we were told to report for our posting.

I was sent to Hawarden with another girl but we were there for only a few weeks and were then posted to Kirton in Lindsey in Lincolnshire. This was a fighter station but not operational. We had a Polish squadron as well as the RAF. The Poles eventually left and were replaced by an American squadron. That certainly livened the place up.

I drove lorries, coaches, vans and ambulances and did my share of cleaning engines. We had a WAAF mess and the food was very good. We were also allowed out until midnight except for domestic evening. We lived in married quarters, eight to a house, three downstairs and five upstairs in two bedrooms. Scunthorpe was our nearest town and buses ran there every evening.

After about a year I managed to get an exchange posting to Tilstock just a couple of miles from my home. For a while I lived on camp, but then I applied to live at home and was granted a living out pass. I cycled to and from home each day. The MT girls were a nice crowd and very friendly. When I arrived, Tilstock was 81 OTU with Wellingtons and Whitley bombers. The driving included flarepath, water wagon, latrine wagon, ambulance and numerous other jobs.

During 1944 the station became 1665 Conversion Unit with

Halifax and Stirling bombers. We also had Horsa gliders. One job I hated was collecting the glider tow ropes after these had been released by the aircraft. I felt that they were always trying to score a direct hit on my vehicle.

One of my saddest jobs was taking a WAAF to a sanatorium in Yorkshire. She was quite ill and said she would be there for at least a year.

In 1945 the Halifaxes and Stirlings left us for a move to another station and we became 81 OTU again with Whitleys and Wellingtons.

MT life was certainly very varied and everyday we drove a different vehicle and travelled around the country. Even though we were grade 5, the lowest pay group, I enjoyed my life in the WAAF.

I met my husband at Tilstock and we were married in December 1945. He was one of the flying instructors, Flight Lieutenant J.L. Suddaby. We are still married and have one son, John, who is now forty years old. I can't beieve it; where have all the years gone?

Every year Peggy Drummond-Hay arranges a reunion at one of the hotels in Whitchurch. We are all very grateful to her for the chance to meet again and reminisce. It makes a lovely weekend and long may it continue!

14

ANNE LEECH (NOW DOUGLAS)

One night I was detailed for flarepath duty at Tilstock and had taken the airmen onto the airfield to lay the flares on the side of the runway. We then made our way to the crew hut to wait for further duties. Sometime during the night a call came from Flying Control to say that the wind had changed direction and we were to go out and onto the runway and change the flarepath as soon as possible as some aircraft were due to return to base very soon. So pronto we chugged away at fifteen miles an hour in the Bantams. All was going smoothly. We were picking up the sodium lights and placing them on the new runway when, suddenly, one of the airmen let out a yell. 'Quick, Jock, there is a b_____ aircraft coming in on this runway.'

They all scooted off the runway, leaving me sitting in the vehicle, and as I looked up I saw the lights of a Stirling ahead. I was panic-stricken but I managed to get my foot well and truly on the accelerator and get clear of the runway just in time!

Another time, whilst on night-flying duty in 'C' Flight, I had taken a corporal out to an aircraft to fit oxygen bottles and I was sitting in my vehicle waiting in the lorry park some way from the aircraft. He seemed much longer doing the job than usual, so I went over to the kite and gave him a call but got no reply. I was feeling rather impatient as I had to shortly drive the aircrew to the cookhouse for their night-flying supper. I climbed inside the aircraft and worked my way up to the cockpit and there I found Corporal Tommy Atkins knocked out on the floor; the oxygen bottle had exploded in his face which was in a terrible mess. I managed to get him out of the aircraft somehow and into my lorry to sick quarters and in the care of a medical orderly. When I came out of SSQ my lorry had disappeared — crikey! In my haste I had not put on the handbrake fully and it had rolled down the bottom of the hill but, fortunately, had been stopped by a tree, beyond which was the Great North Road! (This was at Woolfox Lodge.) I thanked the tree very much for saving the day and no Form 446 had to be filled out!

The corporal was transferred to hospial as there was a danger of him losing his sight, but the accident had a happy ending, as it brought his fiancée back to him after they had recently quarrelled and parted.

Note: Anne married Angus Douglas who was a sergeant in the Electrical Section. He had joined the RAF in 1938, and stayed in after the war till he was demobbed in 1975. They had some interesting overseas postings — Singapore, Malaya, Bahrain and Germany. Angus was with 1665 HCU from 1944 till 1946.

15

PAT HAWKES (NOW STEEL)

I was attending Leamington Spa Business Training College when war broke out in September 1939. By Easter 1940 I had my first job in a solicitor's office but at the end of the year I was offered a job in the livestock office for Warwickshire. This was very interesting but with the blitz on Coventry and surrounding areas, it meant very long working hours, as it entailed visiting farms to assess bomb damage. I shall never forget driving through Coventry (with a special pass) and seeing all the devastation — it was horrific.

After signing up to join the WAAF in 1942 I had to wait for my papers and my call-up was postponed because I got mumps! I eventually arrived at RAF Innsworth on 2 July 1942 and spent four weeks there on square-bashing and innoculation, kitting etc. A week of this was spent in hospital as a result of a bad reaction to the small pox vaccination.

We were then posted to Morecambe where our group were the first batch to do an MT course there. We were billeted in civilian houses at the other end of the town where we had more square-bashing to contend with and more lectures on the RAF. We started our first lessons driving thirty hundred weight lorries which I enjoyed, since I had been driving vehicles since I was seventeen. Many of the girls had never been behind a wheel before so it was rather tough on them.

On passing out as an MT driver, I was posted to Pershore in Worcestershire and then to the satellite station of Atherstone near Stratford-on-Avon. This was great as I was quite close to home and I had an aunt and uncle a couple of miles away and many friends in the area. We had Whitleys and Wellingtons as training aircraft on the airfield and everything was fine for a while. Then early in 1943, I was posted to RAF Tilstock (after Marjorie but before Betty).

At Tilstock initially I was luckily billeted in sick quarters as my duties were to drive the ambulance. I also had to drive a little Hillman van about for the Squadron Leader engineering officer who had his office in a hanger near to the Raven Hotel on the other side of the perimeter track. Having passed a test to drive coaches in Whitchurch, I was made duty crew coach driver with Betty and Marjorie.

Some three experiences come to mind whilst at Tilstock. One frosty morning when on crew coach duty with Betty we took a short cut through the officers' mess entrance to get to the section and I collided with the Roman Catholic padre. We landed together on the ground and he groaned rather loudly when he first got to his feet, so I thought it would be better for me to stay on the ground and make a bit of fuss too! So we were told off for short-cutting through the officers' mess grounds!

Driving one morning to Whitchurch in the small ambulance taking patients to catch a train, and accompanied by Pat Kelly, we met an American Army convoy. The officer in charge of the convoy was in a lorry in the middle of the road. I imagine he wanted to get to the front of the convoy and being on the left hand side it was necessary for him to come right across the road to see if it was clear. Unfortunately, he did this just as we were level with him. He came out into us and hit us. The result was that the ambulance was a write-off and I had to have seven stitches in my head, which hit the windscreen wiper controls. But the American officer came to our MT Section officer and accepted all the blame for the accident.

My other experience was taking an airman to Cosford Hospital in an ambulance that had been in the MT yard for a 500 miles inspection and which I had to use, whether the inspection was completed or not. I heard a noise on the way to Cosford but the airman, who was a stretcher case, arrived at the hospital in good spirits. On the way back my rear wheel suddenly overtook me, and I then knew what the noise had been! Somehow, with the help of a passer by, we managed to get the wheel on again and I returned to camp without further mishap. Sergeant Powell (MT) said that I should have checked the vehicle before I left and put me on a charge. Luckily, the WAAF CO did not agree with him so I was let off.

Just after VE Day I spent a couple of weeks in hospital having impacted wisdom teeth removed but the posting I had applied for to Church Lawton had come through — it was the end of August by then.

Church Lawton was near Rugby and was No. 20 EFTs and also the satellite station to Snitterfield. I had to collect four dead bodies in the small ambulance and I was terrified as I thought that perhaps they could come to life or something on the way!

My boyfriend, Doug, and I had both lived in the village next to Snitterfield camp. We had always kept in touch throughout the war whilst he was in the artillery in North Africa, in the landing on Sicily and the advance to the top of Italy. He came home on leave for a month in September 1945 and I saw him every day when I did the DRLS run daily to Snitterfield with the MT officer's permission. We got engaged and in January 1946 I was promoted to corporal and as there were only six WAAF drivers on camp I spent most of the time in the office doing duty rotas. I was demobbed in September and Doug and I were married on 9 November and lived in Alcester where Doug was in the making-up department of meats at Alcester Co-Operative Society. After a while he found a shop in Stratford which proved very successful until he retired.

Having no family, I was advised to get a job and I became a secretary at the old people's home in Alcester, eventually being up-graded by the administrative side. The home was closed in 1975 and I did the same work in the National Health Service at Stratford Hospital. I retired in 1983 and so we moved to Claverdon which is a lovely village and only four miles from where we were brought up.

I shall never forget the WAAF driver days and the comradeship it brought and lasting friendships.

104

16

BETTY DYSON (NOW AVISON)

When war broke out I was working in an office of a local engineering works. I had no intention of joining up as I had never been away from home before, even on holiday. My parents were more fun to go away with than any of my friends! I was very happy living with them. However, I had no choice in the matter and I was called up on 3 December 1942. Very traumatic, as you can imagine.

I had to report to RAF Innsworth initially and then did my square-bashing at Compton-Bassett near Calne in Wiltshire. Field Marshal Lord Birdwood reviewed our passing out parade. It was December and as we were standing on parade for over two hours, it got distinctly uncomfortable! Then I was posted to Arbroath on the north-east coast of Scotland, on New Year's Eve of all times and it took about twenty four hours to get there! I had to wait there until there was a place on the driving course available. After about three weeks I was posted to RAF Cardington near Bedford for my course — all the way back south again!

Whilst on the square-bashing course, I had made friends with another UT MT girl who had been one of George Black's show girls, but we were separated after the course. I had some big heavy pink bedsocks which I used to pin to my pyjamas. So when I was assigned to a hut after arriving mid-afternoon I made my bed and put my pyjamas and bedsocks on my pillow before going to tea. When I returned my friend was sitting on the next bed. Having just arrived and recognised my bedsocks, she took the next bed to me! We were the only two UT MT girls to be sent to Cardington on the MT course, as all the others went to Weeton.

After I passed out as a fully qualified MT Driver in March 1943, I was posted to RAF Tilstock in Shropshire and stayed there until the end of March 1946 and I was one of the last to leave. I helped to close the station up, which was very depressing as I had had a good time there and made some good friends. I can recall two amusing incidents whilst at Tilstock. The first was when I had to take an aircraft fitter with me to collect some heavy equipment in a small Hillman van. This had to go in the van on the floor behind me. On the way back to camp we were driving through a market town when I had to make an emergency stop — I don't remember what for — and the fitter, who obviously had no confidence in my driving, yanked the handbrake on with all his might, causing all the equipment to slide forward, tilting my seat and pinning me to the windscreen with my face squashed against it! My language to my passenger wasn't very lady-like! What made it worse, was the fact that it took him twenty minutes to remove it — much to the amusement of passers-by who saw my predicament.

The other episode was on pay parade, after I had been in hospital and then on sick leave — five weeks in all. Pay parade was in the MT Section and the MT officer sat in his office and we had to queue outside waiting to be called in to receive our pay. We then marched in smartly and saluted, giving the last three digits of our service number. The sergeant then handed you the money, another salute and about turn for marching out. All very correct and serious. As I hadn't had any pay for a long time, I was expecting quite a large amount but the MT officer simply said, 'ten shillings' — you can imagine my dismay! Whereupon, instead of saluting, taking the money and marching out, I stared at Burne in disbelief and yelled at the top of my voice, 'What!' There was a deathly silence for a few seconds until everyone came too and he just handed me the money and I walked out. Needless to say all the others waiting in the corridor were helpless with laughter and I felt a perfect fool. I received the correct pay the next day, however.

There was an article in the local paper the other day about a Halifax bomber crew who met up again at Tilstock after forty-five years. They had a three day reunion staying at Whitchurch. There were also photos of them then and now. One of the crew lives in Huddersfield and the rest are from Inverness, Essex, Australia and Plymouth. I am writing to the same paper to tell them about our reunions.

17

ROSEMARY HAYES (NOW MACFADYEN)

On Sunday 3 September, when war was declared, I was almost fifteen years old. The first air-raid siren sounded soon after the announcement and my mother became hysterical, pushing me head first into a cupboard under the stairs! My father was very quiet, obviously thinking of his First World War comrades. He had been gassed and had a mosaic design of bullet wounds on both legs. I adored him. He was born in 1878 of Irish parents and christened in the Roman Catholic church of St. James, Spanish Place, London. I know nothing else, except he was fun, and taught me to enjoy the pleasure of walking and seeing the flowers, trees, earth, plus the knowledge that one half of me is conservative English and the other half, fighting Irish, with a tendency to mock authority. My father died the following May and the Battle of Britain started in September when I was sixteen.

Bombs fell close to us and the incendiary bombs were frightening, but my mother and neighbours dashed hither and thither with bowls of water; it was a bit like 'Dads Army', but effective.

When I was seventeen and a half, I had a tremendous fight with my mother when I volunteered to join the WAAF: she thought I would be doomed for ever, and my sister, ten years older, told me not to come home with a baby! Educated by nuns and completely naive, I was almost paranoid about even kissing and I can only speak for myself and friends in MT that we were all unsophisticated.

So on 8 March 1942, with a splendid sense of adventure, I set forth for Bridgenorth in Shropshire, a basic training camp, where we were issued with our uniforms and 'irons'. I remember being embarassed walking about with those eating tools and queueing up for food. None of the sergeants or officers smiled at us, it was all orders and shouting, drill and discipline; the nuns' and my mothers' authority paled in comparison! As I struggled with kit inspection, strangled myself with an alien tie, marched left leg and arm together, so that I looked like a troubled duck, and failed to sleep night after night on my three straw filled biscuits, surrounded by snores, heavy breathing and stifled sobbing, I thought 'Dear God, what have I got into?'

However, at the end of six weeks I began to enjoy it, and felt very proud when I travelled home in uniform with my kitbag, for forty-eight hours leave before going to Morecambe, Lancs for three wonderful months. I was to be a MT Driver. Not many people had cars in the 1930's and the thought of learning to drive was exciting. We were in billets with Morecambe landladies; some were battle axes, but our family, the Taylors, were so kind that none of us wanted to leave them. We had some square-bashing, route marches with hearty singing, and we learnt to drive!

My first vehicle was a Bedford 15 cwt lorry, followed by Fordson lorries and all night convoys. Looking at my September diary, I have just scrawled 'enjoying my MT training but too busy to write in diary'! Then, 'Driving a WOT 3 now and a Commer; it is very bouncy and I feel quite sea-sick — and the gears...!'

I seem to spend most evenings at the Floral Dance Hall or the theatre, where I found my love of drama and music, jazz and classical and it was so cheap. We could afford it even out of our pittance, if we were careful. The beauties of Silverdale and Kendal thrilled me too, and the lovely Lake District, seen in all its glory, without traffic jams.

In November 1942, I was posted to RAF Harwell, OTU Wellingtons. I lived in married quarters, and after a while enjoyed it but I had two mishaps. I was told to collect a car

109

outside No. 3 Hangar. Well, I could not find that particular car all four hangars looked the same. There was a car outside No 1 Hangar and it was not immobilised. True it did not display the right number but I thought someone had made a mistake, so I drove to Sick Quarters, went to Oxford hospital with three patients and had a lovely day wandering around the delights of Oxford. On my return I was arrested at the main gate by two 'red caps' and frog-marched left-right, left-right to Headquarters.

I found myself in front of a visiting Air Marshal who was visiting all Bomber Command Stations in Oxfordshire. My face was a picture of disbelief but I think he had a sneaking sense of humour, because he was, after the first blast, quite kind! Seven days jankers — my first but not my last.

The second mishap involved a 15 cwt Bedford lorry with dodgy gears. I was on the brow of a hill and I wanted to reverse into a track and return to camp the way I had come, to get to this isolated hillock. I could not get into reverse gear and thought that if I took the handbrake off I could push it around. With horror, I watched the vehicle speed downhill, ending up in a ditch. A walk of about seven miles and a confession, more jankers and, worse, I was never allowed to forget it! The 'nasties' — coal or dustbin jobs were always mine — 'give it to bloody Samson', the sergeant would say.

A ballet dancer from Sadlers Wells came to entertain us and we girls of the chorus were told to dance about the stage like falling leaves — he was dancing to something called 'Trees'. Thanks to stodgy food and NAAFI wads, we were anything but waif-like and resembled falling branches rather than drifting leaves. The audience loved it, laughing, whistling and shouting unmentionable comments — not all of them had seen a male ballet dancer in all his glory!

More trouble and another posting, this time to RAF Tilstock, Prees Heath, 81 OTU Whitley or flying coffins as they were often called. It would have been a wonderful place for a sanatorium for consumptives: a forest of pine trees and silver birch, the air pine fresh and sweet. We were issued with bicycles;

they were the only means of transport. The ablutions were prehistoric and it was so cold we had tide marks round our necks for the lack of hot water! The most popular job was the crew coach; that was the glamour job taking the aircrew out to their 'kites' and, on their return, back to the debriefing room.

Sometime later we were invaded by 1665 HCU. At the time I had been posted once again, to the satellite station RAF Sleap. When booking out of the guardroom at Tilstock, we always had the tired old joke, 'going to Sleap with six officers then?' Pat Kelly, bless her, I'm sure, always replied, 'I am going to Sleap, Sergeant!' I say that because in one sentence, Pat could use six unpronounceable words that we had not heard of before; it encouraged me to buy a dictionary.

At Sleap I was on flarepath duty driving a 3 ton Albion and my partner on the trafficator vehicle was Vera. She always wore an old leather jacket and we used to joke with her saying, 'you will die in that old jerkin, take it off'. One late afternoon, I reversed under the wing of a Whitley and ran over a bicycle and a few days later I went back to Tilstock to face another charge and stayed the night there. Another nineteen year old, a pretty girl named Kitty had taken over my duties in the Albion. The next day we awoke in the billet to hear that Vera and Kitty had been killed in the watchtower whilst awaiting the return of the Whitleys, one of which had crashed into the control tower on landing, and all the crew were lost. We were terribly shocked and I had the feeling, 'there for the Grace of God go I,' for we were all aware of the dangers of driving on the airfield especially at night. We did not have headlights, just narrow slits, so it was dark, lonely and the planes taking off and landing were unpredictable — some did crash or swing off the runway. Vera and Kitty live in our memories and as long as we live will not be forgotten.

I also remember the Canadian pilot I drove to Chester Cemetery, his coffin covered with the Union Jack. There was a firing squad and German prisoners leaning on their spades and just the vicar and me.

Most of us lost boyfriends. In our hut there was always drama, that's why we remain such close friends after so many years.

111

The agony of being young!

I returned to Sleap only to be given the job of driving the sanitary wagon. The vehicle was a carrier Bantam; it had a snub nose and an open flat back, and the cramped cabin had a small trap door in the roof. Sleap did not have main drainage and I had to drive around the camp collecting buckets from the loos. There was a corporal in charge and two men in the back sharing bucket space. Now I must confess to being the driver who ditched the vehicle and buckets. It was not an accident but fully intended. One hot day, I decided to take action. Putting the brake on hard I said to the corporal. 'If you touch me again or poke me in the ribs, I am going to ditch this thing!' Well he did and I did, stepping hard on the accelerator I charged hard for the ditch! The poor boys in the back were covered, indeed one had a bucket over his head! The corporal had his head through the trap door stuck fast! Bruised but triumphant, I walked to my billet, changed out of battle dress, climbed through the perimeter fence and went to Shrewsbury. Of course I was on another charge and this time stayed at Tilstock until we all moved to RAF Saltby in March 1945.

But I must not forget Arnhem because that was a most momentous time for us. Our aircrew and the Stirling Bombers towed the gliders with paratroopers on board and also dropped supplies from 17 until 21 September 1944. In four days we had lost so many aircraft and crews that we had two coaches on a shuttle service to replace them.

Sergeant Porter (WAAF) knew my Canadian boyfriend was at RAF Keevil and as it was my birthday, kindly sent me on one of the coaches as the driver, but sadly he had not returned from operations. Raymond Lamont was named at the RAF Memorial Runnymede, 'no known grave'. My husband Archie Ross MacFadyen, was one of the lucky ones — he did survive — but we did not meet until we moved once again to RAF Marston Moor in 1945, when I was driving a troop-carrier taking sixteen officers to York. We were both posted to RAF Linton-on-Ouse and demobilised in July 1946. He went home to Scotland for a while, then came south and we married in 1948.

Thanks to Peggy Drummond-Hay for keeping us together

for so many happy reunions and looking forward to many more where we raise our glasses to the lost ones, especially Vera, Kitty and Dilys

Note: Dilys died about eight years ago of cancer. The first one of us survivors to die which was a shock to us all. She was not very old when she died and served with us on 81 OTU and never married.

18

RAY GLASS, SQUADRON LEADER

10 May 1943 — 8 May 1945

On leaving 241(FMS) Squadron, having completed a second tour of Bomber Operations on Short Stirling Aircraft, I was posted to Waterbeach to form 1665 HCU moving to Woolfox Lodge as OCD Flight converting crews to Stirlings for 3 Group Bomber Command.

Other than the usual flying duties, I was lumbered with being bar officer and Flight Lieutenant Bunny Austin (my second in command) was messing officer. In all it was a pleasant duty squeezing booze out of the local Stamford Brewery and the NAAFI at Grantham for titbits for tea such as marmite for sandwiches. Stamford boasted about a hundred pubs but we never got round to them all! The Ram Jam on the A1, then the Great North Road was a particular favourite being so near to camp. On 13 July 1943 I attended the investiture of my DFC by King George VI at Buckingham Palace.

On learning of our move to Tilstock, I was dispatched to Grantham NAAFI to persuade them to allow us a dozen bottles of Scotch. They said that they could only spare ten bottles but, on opening the crate, we found there were indeed twelve; so then on I was known as 'Two Bottle Glass'! I was also able to procure an eighteen gallon cask from the famous brewers of Bass at Burton-on-Trent which, when empty, had to be sent back by rail to the brewery with a special label on it: 'War Time

Shortages'. The party ended with a number of officers piling furniture up in the centre of the room and, with blackened soles of soot on their feet, walking up the walls and over the ceiling as if someone had actually done it! Of course, the next morning the station commander ordered the culprits to clean the marks off, which they did at lunch time when the mess was full.

The move to Tilstock went well but on my first flight there, on approaching land, wheels were selected down, but one green light would not come on. After several low passes over Flying Control, we were given permission to land on the grass. Fortunately the offending wheel held and was found to be an electrical fault. We now came under 38 Group and the task was to build a force for D-Day to convert crews to towing-duties of Horsa Gliders and for container dropping. As none of us had experience in towing gliders, the Wing Commander Flying and myself flew over Sleap (near Wem) to get some gen from the Whitley boys who were towing there. We hooked up a Horsa to our Stirling and found it no trouble although we had been naturally anxious at first. So onto training on 30 April 1944.

In order to give the crews 'fighter affiliation' experience, and as the fighter squadrons were too busy to do the task, as they were on softening up operations in the Channel, Flying Officer Doug Baker and myself took two week's conversion course onto Hurricanes at No. 5 (PAFJ) at Ternhill. This ensured that the training was completed by 25 August 1944.

On the domestic side, Wing Commander Tomkins, our senior engineering officer, always asked new ground crew their trade in civvy street so that any extraneous jobs around the camp could be done properly. One result was a magnificent stone fireplace in the officers' mess.

During May I was sent on an accident prevention course at Watchfield, the Flying Control school. Ironically, whilst I was there two of my pilots were killed gaining experience in the Horsa Glider which hit the Drem wires on landing. The loss of Bunny Austin and another was tragic.

By D-Day, we had about sixty crews trained standing by to be deployed if required; only a few were needed. We were invited to Great Dunmow to watch the take-off, which defies description!

One of the Stirling went U/S and the troops in their gliders almost went berserk as they thought they would miss the 'show'.

Arnhem was, however, a different kettle of fish and all the crews were deployed. On 1 March Halifaxes arrived on the station and conversion continued. Then we moved to RAF Saltby in Yorkshire. During my time at Tilstock, I was well served by the MT Section, headed by Flight Lieutenant Burne and forty-five years later I attended a reunion of that section at Whitchurch, near Tilstock, and thoroughly enjoyed meeting the 'Master' and his girls, organised by the author of *The Driving Force*!

19

BOB TWEDDLE

One night in November. One morning in May

I had three older brothers, all serving in HM Forces during the Second World War. Sidney was five years older than me and he had left his trainee-solicitor occupation in late 1941 to join the Royal Air Force as a member of Aircrew.

Our family knew he was progressing through his flying training, but never knew he had started on his 'operational' flying in four-engined Halifax bombers. Perhaps he didn't wish to worry our parents at the time.

I was at home with my sister, my younger brother, and my parents when the telegram arrived just after 9.00 pm on 23 November 1943. Needless to say, it was shattering news. The telegram stated 'Killed in Action as the result of Air Operations on the night of 22 November'.

A letter from his commanding officer of 77 Squadron based at RAF Elvington, near York, dated 23 November, told us that Sid's aircraft had completed its operation and whilst flying over this country, had collided with another aircraft and crashed. All on board perished.

He enclosed the names and home addresses of all Sid's crew and suggested my parents might like to get in touch with them.

One of my brother's aircrew was another local man, a Sidney Elder. The two coffins were returned to Carlisle and, by the parents' agreement, were buried side by side in Kingstown War

Graves plot. The officiating vicar, the Rev. Bancroft buried them just a few yards from his own son's grave. He had buried his son, killed in a Beaufighter crash on 16 November, only a few days before.

My father did write to the parents of the other members of the crew, one of whom was a Scotsman. None of the English parents were told just where the crash had occurred, but for some reason the Scottish parents had been given the site as being in the parish of Barmby Moor, near York.

I volunteered in late 1945 and joined the RAFVR in early 1946. I had hoped to be trained as Aircrew but there was no longer any need for such training. The RAF was contracting quickly.

In mid 1946 I was stationed, for a short while, at RAF Dalton. Whilst there I 'borrowed' a bike and cycled down to Barmby Moor. I visited the little burial ground near the church, where around fifty aircrew are interred, then I ferreted out the local policeman. He was such a kindly man and he said that he would have liked to have helped me locate the site of the crash, but he said that there were so many of them in that area that he just couldn't recall them all, let alone any particular one. I cycled back to RAF Dalton and let the matter rest.

Sometime in 1983 I met up with a young man who told me that he could supply the squadron codes and aircraft serial numbers of the two Halifaxes involved in the collision. Later on he told me, in writing, that they were both Mk II's. My brother's aircraft was K-King of 77 Squadron KN-K No. LW264, based at RAF Elvington. The other aircraft was also a K-King, DY-K No. LW 333 based at 102 Squadron at RAF Pocklington. The two stations were fairly close to one another. The time of the crash was 23.55 hours.

Both aircraft were made by the English Electric Company and must have been only two to three months old when they crashed. They were both part of Contract No. ACFT/1808.

I filed this information away.

In May of 1984 my wife and I were holidaying in the Yorkshire area, staying at bed and breakfast establishments which caught our interest. After visiting Castle Howard we dropped down to Barmby Moor village and visited the church and the now immaculate RAF burial ground.

By the time we had walked around, it was getting on for 6.00 p.m. and I was rather taken aback to see that most of the obvious B & B's were booked and showed the 'No Vacancies' signs.

We decided to motor towards York, looking for somewhere to stay the night in the country but prepared to find something in York City, if necessary.

Driving along the York Road we spotted a sign on the lefthand side, nailed on a tree on the junction of a lane. It read 'Farmhouse B & B 300 Yards Up Lane'. We turned in and drove up to a lovely little farm house. I popped in, met a delightful Mrs Scott, and learned she had a room available. The farm was then known as Newlands Farm, now called the Mohair Farm.

The room was beautifully comfortable and we were very impressed. The view out of our bedroom window was across some of their fields and we watched the rabbits playing in the evening sunshine.

We slept comfortably and well and we decided to ask if we could stay on for another night. Mrs Scott served us our breakfast, a smashing meal, and we asked if this was possible. She agreed but asked us if we could find our way back again, after our proposed day in York. I told this young woman that I did know the area, that we would be able to find our way back again, and then mentioned I'd lost a brother somewhere in the vicinity, during the war, when two Halifaxes collided and fell.

She rather astounded me when she pointed out of the breakfast room window to the same field we viewed from our bedroom, and told us that two Halifaxes had fallen in that very field. She pointed out the different colour of the grass, and where a length of hedgerow had been replaced by a barbed wire fence. Mrs Scott wasn't born until well after the war so everything she told us was 'second-hand' from her husband's family. She told us it was said to have been a foggy night late on in the year.

We went off to York to visit the Jorvik Viking Centre and returned to our 'billet' on a lovely sunny evening. My wife went in to clean up and I asked if I could walk our dogs on this, and

119

the adjoining field which had just been ploughed. I was quite amazed to see quite a number of pieces of aluminium and fragments of perspex. They were all small in size but remarkably clean, and the metal was almost shiny. I picked a few pieces up and popped them into my pocket. I've still got them.

I couldn't help but think this might well have been the very site of my brother's death. I just felt inside of me that this WAS the place and I mentally ridiculed myself for thinking this way.

We spoke again to Mrs Scott, asking if there was anything else she could recall of the field's history. She told us that a few years back a group of men had arrived at the farm, armed with a metal detector. They told her and her husband that they were an aircraft archaeology research unit, based on RAF Linton-on-Ouse and they told her of their wish to recover a Merlin engine which was thought to be buried in the field. They asked permission to start a dig. Permission was given but no Merlin was found, so they departed. I decided to approach the commanding officer of RAF Linton-on-Ouse on my return home.

I did so in early June of 1984. I told the officer commanding, group Captain P. J. Kemp everything I knew.

The group captain passed my letter onto the gentleman who was in charge of the Linton Memorial Room, a certain William Steel of New Earswick, who combined that post with being a bit of an historian of 'all things RAF' in that area. Bill, who I regret to say died earlier in 1992, wrote to me. After a period of time to check through the existing historical records, he wrote again to confirm that Newlands Farm was the 'last resting place' of the aircraft. He also told me that the station never ever had an aircraft archaeology research group so it would appear that the so-called 'team' were probably freelancers who spun that yarn to get permission to dig.

I relayed copies of letters to Mrs Scott for information, and it was she who suggested planting an oak tree in memory of my brother's crew of seven. It was Bill Steel's wisdom which suggested two such trees, one for each aircrew.

I was determined that my family would foot the bill for the two trees, so I put my suggestion to my eldest brother, Douglas, my sister Elizabeth and my younger brother, Norman. All wished to share the cost.

Douglas was an 'old' Lancaster pilot of No. 9 Squadron. He survived over forty operations and emerged a Bomber Command 'survivor' with a DFC for three Tirpitz bombing raids. His health wasn't too good at the time.

We decided that we would finance fourteen little oak trees, one for each of the two crews.

This information I passed on to Mrs Scott who told me that as there was a large number of young oak trees growing on the farm, there was no need to buy any 'outsiders'!

It was she who agreed with me that we could plant them on the farm, on 22 November 1984. She suggested she would mention the planting to the Yorkshire Post and Yorkshire TV.

Group Captain P.J. Kemp organised three young pilots to show up at the 'ceremony'. A flagpost was erected and the flag flown. The local Barmby Moor vicar came along and said a few suitable words. Quite a crowd of other folk appeared, some who had lost brothers, fathers and boyfriends flying out of four group bomber bases. It was all a rather emotional time, especially when we asked if some of those attending wished to plant one of the trees. There were a lot of damp sparkling eyes.

The young pilots did expert work planting a tree each. They did equally expert work opening some wine bottles at our little party held in Mrs Scott's home afterwards. Come to think of it they were pretty good emptying the glasses. It was a damp drizzling morning. Real Yorkshire weather for that time of the year. When it was all over we broke up.

I am pleased to say that my younger brother, plus his wife, my sister and myself were all able to attend, but Douglas, the Lancaster pilot, had just had a heart attack and wasn't up to the journey. I regret to say that his health never allowed him to make the journey to Yorkshire. He died several months later.

As a result of the publicity I received a number of letters. One was from a chap called Slaughter. He had been in the National Fire Service and his team had been called out to the crash site. He sent me a copy of Form Pad K 4T8, on which all the details were noted down. His team was called out at 0007

121

hours on 23 November.

His report states: 'RAF Personnel. Occupants of Planes. Names Unknown. 14 in number. All Dead.'

The Public Record Office furnished me with all the names. They were: Halifax II No. LW264 'K' of 77 Squadron RAF Elvington: Flight Sergeant C.C. Lineham, Sergeant A.D. West, flight Sergeant E.B. Gosden, Sergeant S. Tweddle, Sergeant S. Elder, Sergeant J.L. Bennet, Sergeant W.G. Thomson. Halifax II No. LW 333 'K' of I02 Squadron RAF Pocklington: Pilot Officer W. Hughes, Sergeant W.W. Cottle, Sergeant R.A. Dabnor, Sergeant R.B. Bainbridge, Flight Sergeant D. Willington, Sergeant J. Boxall, Sergeant F.T. Dunn.

If any reader recognises a name in this list and wishes to contact me, please do so.

Lastly, but certainly not the least emotional letter I received was from a lady in York.

She told me that she had been Sid's girlfriend for a short while before his death. She mentioned names in her letter which only Sid could have told her, so she was absolutely genuine.

They had made a date to meet next time in York. She always wondered why he never turned up to keep it, but had no way of knowing the true reason until she read her *Yorkshire Post* of 23 November 1984.

I rang her after reading her letter. Even after all those forty one years she could describe his appearance, and it was all too obvious that he had meant a great deal to her. She had never forgotten him. I will never forget her, or all the other kindly folk who, just because of a few words spoken on a morning in May, helped to put together this story.

20

JOHN MARTIN

How I won the OBE

I heard the swish of the Grim Reaper's scythe at Flying Control
Sleap in the early hours of a September morning in 1943, while
on duty as a radiotelephony (RT) operator. Fortunately it missed
me by a few yards but sadly it cut down nine young lives.

Strictly speaking, I was a wireless operator awaiting aircrew
training as a W/T observer but had been posted to Tilstock with
the advice to get as much experience as possible on all aspects
of signals work before going on a navigation course.

In June, Flying Control at Tilstock were short of an RT
operator and I was ordered to report to the senior control officer,
Squadron Leader Yule. My mild protests that I hadn't a clue
concerning an RT op's duties were swept aside with a 'Now's
your chance to learn, laddie!' At the watch office I was put in
the care of a grizzled old veteran named Corporal Batchelor.
'Batch' condensed the normal six week course of training for
an RT operator into about six hours dual instruction, after which
he and Squadron Leader Yule approved me going solo. My
membership of the flying control team lasted about two months
until a regular RT operator was posted to us and then it was
back to SHQ signals for me.

It was, therefore, no surprise when we received an urgent
request from Sleap Flying Control, towards the end of August,
for an RT operator that I was promptly despatched. The reason

for my hasty transfer from Tilstock to Sleap was because the operator I was replacing had been injured. A Whitley bouncing on landing and swinging off the runway, had crashed into the control tower, killing the pilot and bomb aimer and injuring the rest of the crew, as well as some of the personnel in the watch office.

I well remember, on my first watch at Sleap, seeing what had been a large hole in the control room wall caused by the port engine of the unlucky Whitley two days before. This had already been bricked up. I had the comforting thought, 'Well, lightning doesn't strike twice in the same place, so that won't happen again.' In less than two weeks I was to be proved terribly wrong.

I was on an evening tour of duty from 17.00 to 23.00 which was passing peacefully enough, when about half an hour before I was due to go off watch, a message came through to expect possible diversions of bombers returning from operations in the early hours, whose bases would be closed down due to bad weather.

Flight Lieutenant Mattingley, the control officer, came over to me and asked if I would go to the mess for a late supper at 23.00 and return as soon as possible to be on standby, in case the diversions materialised and a 'flap' developed. In this event, I was to take over the RT from my relieving operator who was not too experienced. He suggested that I got my head down in the small rest room and promised that I would not be called for unless it was deemed necessary.

Returning to control from supper at about 23.45, I met our Canadian control officer, Flying Officer Brooks, who was now on duty for the night and he confirmed that he knew about the standby arrangements. He was chatting to two pretty young WAAFs who, I think, were the duty MT drivers. I proceeded up the stairs to the rest room on the first floor and had some difficulty in pushing open the door and could only close it after me by giving it a hefty slam.

Little did I realise at that time what a deadly pattern Fate was weaving for me. First my crash course at Tilstock to enable me to be an efficient RT operator, then the accident at Sleap, necessitating my transfer thereto, then being obliged to stay on duty after my evening watch had been completed and finally a sticking door!

The night was so warm so I drew the blackout curtain and opened the small window before lying, fully clothed, on top of the bed. I didn't sleep but lay listening to the RT chatter coming over the loudspeaker in the main control room, which was quite audible.

I suppose it must have been soon after midnight when I heard the voice of the airfield controller, 'Freshfield U 'Uncle' taking off'. Then the roaring crescendo of two Merlin engines as a Whitley revved up for maximum power to get its heavy bulk off the ground. The sound seemed to be getting very near! Suddenly an urgent warning shout over the loudspeaker, 'Look out, control, he's heading for you', followed immediately by a tremendous crunching explosion. The whole building shuddered and night was turned into day as a vast conflagration ensued. Obviously 'U-Uncle' had swung on take-off and bull-dozed into the tower.

I rushed to the door; it wouldn't open! I had no way of knowing whether the exit from the stairs was blocked by flaming wreckage or even if the building was on fire and about to collapse. There was only one thing to do — bale out through the window. Jamming my cap on my head (why, I shall never know) I pushed off hard with my right foot on the sill, to clear bicycles parked below, thudded to earth in a muddy patch and rolled over. Getting shakily to my feet, I felt a twinge of pain in my back, which I must have jarred.

Running around to the crash area, a horrific scene met my eyes. The aircraft had ploughed into the ground floor of the watch office and burst into flames. The crash and fire parties were doing all that was humanly possible but it was obvious that the only possible survivor might be the rear gunner who was furthest from the point of impact. Happily he was eventually extracted from his turret.

I approached Flying Officer Brooks who was visibly distressed, but it was not until I heard him say, in an agonised voice, 'Oh my God! Those two poor girls,' that I realised the WAAFs on MT duty had been in the room which had taken the full force of the collision. I only hoped that they had been killed instantly before being engulfed by hundreds of gallons of flaming, high-octane petrol.

I asked Flying Officer Brooks if there was anything I could do but he said, 'There's no point in you hanging around here lad, you're on watch at 08.00, so get back to your hut and catch up on some sleep.' Sleep was, of course, impossible, partly due to the pain in my back but mainly because of the carnage I had so narrowly escaped and the terrible fate of the two girls kept swirling around in my mind.

With some difficulty, I got off my bed at about 06.30. Our hut NCO Corporal Swettenham, was very concerned at my condition and suggested that I reported sick but this seemed out of the question. Old 'Sweat', as we called him, worked in the clothing stores and was aghast at the sight of my liberally mud-stained uniform. The next day he replaced this with a new one so I ended up with two 'best blues'. After a wash and shave, I limped into the mess for breakfast. News of the tragic events earlier that morning had spread round the camp and a few verbal compliments addressed to me, such as 'Good show, son' or 'Well done, lad' cheered me up somewhat, as I joined the queue.

I had just received a sausage and some tomato on my tin plate when a motherly looking WAAF corporal, supervising the serving counter, beckoned me over. 'Were you involved in the prang at Flying Control'? she asked. I confirmed that I had been. 'Hang on a minute,' she said. Whether she felt I should receive some reward to compensate me for my harrowing experience or whether the sight of a small, dishevelled airman in a dirty uniform evoked pangs of pity in her ample bosom, I shall never know, but the kind soul soon returned with a plate on which shone two fried eggs underlined with a large rasher of streaky bacon.

I had been presented with the OBE — the Order of Bacon and Eggs!

CONTACTS

When reading some of the old letters I have come across, I thought I'd try and contact an Australian pilot I knew at Woolfox Lodge. My husband was a bit sceptical about this as he had flown with many Aussies during the war and found some of them a bit wild! I had remembered Ron's address, as it was written on the back of the food parcels sent to him from Australia which I used to collect for him when he was on late flying.

I managed to obtain his phone number from enquiries which proved he was still alive. That was the easy part of the exercise because I had to decide whether to phone him or not. After several weeks I phoned and he answered straight away, which took us both by surprise, so I told him who I was and there was complete silence. I think he thought I was some kind of quizz or crank phoning! I repeated my name: 'Peggy, an MT driver on the crew coach at Woolfox Lodge'. He then remembered, but I knew his mind was racing back in time to put a face to the name. He gave me his postal address so I could write.

It was great to know that he and his crew had survived the war and we corresponded for about three years before we went on holiday to Australia. In 1991 we spent nine most enjoyable days with him and his charming wife, Shirley, at their home in Perth. They were marvellous hosts and had two parties in our honour to meet other members of his old squadron and their wives. Their squadron was 196 after they left Woolfox Lodge HCU. It was a great thrill to meet them after forty-seven years and we are hoping that Ron and Shirley will stay with us in

Selsey when they come to the UK. We spent six weeks in Australia and travelled nearly 6,000 miles but did not climb Ayers Rock, although I had my birthday there! We thought it was a vast and lovely country.

I also had known a Canadian at Woolfox Lodge and thought it would be a good idea to make contact so I could find out what happened to him and his crew. As I belong to the Stirling Association, I phoned Grace Panichelli of the editorial staff to see if they had his address on their Canadian branch computer sheet and so they had. This time I wrote and eventually had a long reply from a delighted Vernon. He is now a widower but still very actively concerned with the Lancasters over there and flies with them on various demonstrations at air shows. He had gone onto Lancasters after his Stirling crew had been shot down. Luckily he hadn't been flying on that mission, due to a heavy cold. He then went onto 7 Squadron Path Finders at RAF Oakington.

Since I started writing this book, I can now add that in June 1992 we visited Canada and during our seven weeks, we stayed four days with Vernon. We all went to Winnipeg for a week to attend the Sixth Commonwealth Air Crew Reunion. Some four thousand attended with wives and much to Peter's delight, he met up with three of his old crew (Canadians) that he had not seen or heard of for forty-seven years.

Luckily my husband does not mind me making these contacts as he is very interested to hear about their well-being and their service background. He has been a great help in writing this small book and has censored some of my wanderings which made me appear to be boy-mad! It was, of course, difficult to avoid men driving the crews about the airfields and I wasn't the only WAAF on the station! I am sure there are many WAAF drivers who served on fully operational fighter and bomber airfields, who could tell more interesting stories than I have. We only served the Bomber boys when they were on training units, but it niggled us a bit to be only Class 5 grade in the WAAF, as we took our lives into our hands on many occasions, especially night, driving on the airfield with masked lights admidst all the confusion of aircraft taxi-ing (without lights!) and the general

128

roar of their engines confusing the issue further. Luckily, my mother had no idea what went on on the airfield, nor off it!

Whilst at one of the Stirling Association reunions I was talking to Jack Carey who had been on Stirlings and he told me about an amusing incident that happened to him on a night-flying test:

'In early 1944 I was stationed at Mepal with 75 NZ Squadron and on 8 February was detailed to do a night-flying test on LJ 457. It so happened that some half-dozen airmen needed a visit to Woolfox Lodge so I duly landed there in the afternoon. After half an hour or so they returned and I prepared to start up. Starting on batteries-port inner first no problem, starboard inner next no joy. The starter motor was u/s.'

'At the time, Woolfox Lodge had no units in residence so no assistance of any kind was available but one of the passengers was the engineering leader and he had an idea! A length of long rope suddenly appeared, a loop was tied in one end and duties apportioned. The mid-upper gunner was stationed in the fuselage to prime as necessary; I stayed at the controls and the flight engineer had the dubious privilege of sitting astride the engine nacelle twenty feet above the tarmac and gingerly stretching forward each time the loop needed slipping over the blade of the propeller. Everyone else pulled, whereupon the prop would each time turn one third of a circle. A slow job and after six or more attempts, apparently futile, the engine fired; the rope fell off and my engineer was blown off! The other engines started all right and we were back at Mepal as darkness fell.'

APPENDIX ONE

Marjorie had kept all her notes taken whilst on her MT course. I have copied a few of the regulations. How she managed to keep such a neat and tidy book is still beyond me, no wonder my book was mainly blank and certainly not worth keeping.

Wartime Regulations for Lights on Vehicles

A sidelight must not show any light except towards the front. The aperture must not be more than one inch in diameter and must be covered with the equivalent of two thick meshes of newspaper so that the light is clearly visible from 30 yards and invisible from 300 yards.

A tail-lamp must not show any light except a red light towards the rear; the aperture must not exceed one inch in diameter.

Headlights must be fitted with the regulation masking screen so that no light is thrown outside a radius of 15 feet. Power of the headlight bulbs must not exceed a power of 36 watts.

APPENDIX TWO

Have You Done Your Daily Inspection?

1. Check the radiator is full.
2. Check the contents of the fuel tank. Note the capacity of the tank is 7¼ galls.
3. Check the oil level in the engine sump and top up as necessary with oil-stores, ref 344/35.
4. Examine the engine, gearbox and fuel system visually for leaks.
5. Start the engine and ensure the carburettor starting control is not sticking. Note: if the engine has not been run for ten days or more operate the priming lever on the fuel pump until the float chamber is full. Remove the spark plugs and inject a small quantity of oil into each cylinder and turn the engine over by hand ten times!
6. See that the oil pressure indicator is operating properly.
7. See that the speedometer is not damaged.
8. Test the tyre pressures by gauge.
9. Test the operation of the handbrake separately. See that when each brake is fully on the pedal (or lever) is not at the end of its run.
10. Test the operation of the horn, lights, headlamps, dipping system, traffic indicators, windscreen wipers, stop light and all switches.

Sign the Maintenance Book — Form 656 after the necessary entries.

APPENDIX THREE

Types of Vehicle Driven by WAAFS

Standard van, Hillman van, Hillman staff car, Vauxhall car, Humber Snipe shooting brake, 15 cwt Commar, 15 cwt Bedford, 30 cwt Fordson, Bantam carrier, ambulance, 3 ton Fordson coach, 3 ton Bedford trooper, 3 ton left-hand drive Dodge crew coach, 3 ton Albion, de-icing vehicles.

Speed Limits for Vehicles

Types of Vehicle	Economical speed (mph)	Speed not to be Exceeded
Motor Cycle	50—55	60
Cars 8—10 hp	42—45	45
14 hp	45—50	55
Over 14 hp	55—60	60
Trucks 8,12,15 cwt	35—40	40
Lorries 30 cwt	30	30
3 tons	20	20
6 tons	20	20

WAAF MT Drivers also had to do 500 and 2,000 mile inspections in the dreaded pits in the MT yard. They also had to deal with various forms such as some quoted below:

F 446 — Accident procedure

F656 — Daily maintenance form

F 658 — Application for mechanical transport for a service journey

F 814 — A Record of runs carried out whilst at another unit

F 260 — Route form showing destination and stops for fuel and times of arrival and departure, type of load carried and route driven

F 531 — Purchase order, enabling driver to purchase fuel as arranged before leaving the station at pool depot. This form must be signed by the CO of unit and state amounts drawn.

F 666 — Contractors Bill (Blue) to enable driver to purchase spares and have repairs carried out in an emergency.

APPENDIX FOUR

Some Don'ts for MT Drivers

DON'T agitate the accelerator pedal up and down when starting the engine; on most vehicles this upsets the starting mixture.

DON'T keep pulling the starter knob after the engine has started!

DON'T drive with the choke out, push it in as soon as possible.

DON'T top up the radiator with any old rubbish if your vehicle has anti-freeze, top it up with this mixture only; if filled with water, use soft water whenever possible. Remove foreign bodies from stream or pond water.

DON'T pour cold water into a heated or over heated radiator; let it cool first.

DON'T imagine that a 'NO WATER' board is hung on the bonnet for fun!

DON'T dip the oil when the engine is running or when it has just stopped as the dipstick will not tell the truth!

DON'T continue to run the engine when the oil pressure guage reads zero or with the warning light on. The engine may be dangerously short of oil.

DON'T close the reserve petrol tank lever after use when you have refilled the tank normally.

DON'T 'coast' out of gear, the brakes may not be as good — there is a good reason for using the correct gear!

DON'T TURN THE STEERING WHEEL WHILE THE

VEHICLE IS STATIONARY.
DON'T get the idea that maintenance is for other drivers' guidance, the schedule was especially compiled for you!
DON'T assume that because you are a good driver you will never have an accident. Remember the fool round the corner and be extra careful!

Were we overpaid?

Daily Pay

When I first joined the WAAF after training, I was paid 3s. 4d (about 17 new pence) — on 30 December 1945 I had an increase to 4s. 2d.(about 21 new pence). On 1 July 1946 to demob, I received 4s. 10d. (about 24 new pence) a day!